The Divided Heart

Essays on Protestantism and the Enlightenment in America

Henry F. May

New York   Oxford
Oxford University Press
1991

Oxford University Press

Oxford   New York   Toronto
Delhi   Bombay   Calcutta   Madras   Karachi
Petaling Jaya   Singapore   Hong Kong   Tokyo
Nairobi   Dar es Salaam   Cape Town
Melbourne   Auckland

and associated companies in
Berlin   Ibadan

Copyright © 1991 by Henry F. May

Published by Oxford University Press, Inc.,
200 Madison Avenue, New York, New York 10016

Library of Congress Cataloging-in-Publication Data
May, Henry Farnham, 1915-
The divided heart : essays on Protestantism and the Enlightenment
in America / Henry F. May.
p.   cm.   Includes index.   ISBN 0-19-505899-2
1. United States—Religion. 2. Religion and state—United States.
3. Enlightenment. 4. United States—Intellectual life—18th
century. I. Title.
BL2525.M38 1991   291'.0973—dc20   90-40001

9 8 7 6 5 4 3 2 1

Printed in the United States of America
on acid-free paper

For Kenneth M. Stampp,
Colleague and Friend

Acknowledgments

I should like to thank Sheldon Meyer for his support of this project, and Leona Capeless for her sensitive and intelligent editorial suggestions. Those who helped with individual essays are thanked in the editorial notes. I have made minor alterations from the original versions of a number of the essays.

Contents

The Divided Heart

Introduction:
Faith in History[1]

All but one of these essays have been written since 1981. All but the last were written on assigned topics, in answer to specific invitations. Yet as I read them over, all deal either with America's Protestant roots and their survival, or with the eighteenth-century Enlightenment in which the Republic was conceived. Most of the essays, including the more-or-less autobiographical pieces in the first section, touch on the unresolved conflict between these two major forces: hence, the volume's title.

I also find that most if not all the essays seem to bear on a few major questions, recently much discussed, about historical writing. I have usually stayed away from arguments about historiography and philosophy of history. My reluctance to get involved has not been because of any contemptuous dismissal of the inescapable problems with which all historians have to wrestle in their daily work. Rather, it has been because I have little aptitude for abstract thought and have wanted to put in my energies working on specific episodes in the past, treating general historical problems only as they come up in particular contexts.

There is also a deeper reason, a reason rising from my temperament and from certain basic assumptions, made often subconsciously in the process of my work. I approach history, as I approach life itself, with a combination of faith and skepticism. I have never really been able to believe that one can get at a consistent structure of truth either through a syllogistic process, or by making a clear and rational choice between competing alternatives. Still less have I been able to accept any requirement that one must wait until some such process is completed before writing anything. I tried when I was an undergraduate to force myself to make this sort of decision and quickly found that I could not, and that the effort was, for me, destructive. I gave up grand philosophy because I had to. Since then, I have assumed in action (and writing is a form of action) that it is necessary to give one's loyalty to the most plausible and compelling hypothesis, and that which hypothesis one finds compelling is a matter not just of thinking but rather of one's whole life experience. I think I realize the intellectual unsatisfactoriness of this sort of attitude, and I am aware of its many dangers, but I cannot operate in any other way.[2]

Of course I have been aware at many times of the intellectual warfare raging all around me over such matters as historical method, the nature of historical truth, and the political and philosophical message history teaches. When I was in graduate school, the rather worn-out positivist assumptions derived from nineteenth-century science and social science were still dominant. If you did your research carefully and impartially, humbly (or sometimes in practice not so humbly) contributing your factual bit to to the total of historical knowledge, the pattern would somehow, eventually, automatically emerge. My teachers were deeply upset when this view was powerfully challenged in 1943 by the presidential address of Charles A. Beard, which argued that something called "frames of reference" were inescapable and that written history depended on nothing less shocking

4

than an "act of faith." Early on some had already been bothered by Carl Becker's more extreme but less combatively argued relativist doctrine. In *his* presidential address of 1931, Becker had jauntily announced that history was "an imaginative creation, a personal possession which each one of us, Mr. Everyman, fashions out of his individual experience, adapts to his practical or emotional needs, and adorns as well as may be to suit his esthetic taste." It is not surprising that my teachers were upset; these heresies seemed to take all the seriousness and much of the meaning out of the patient, honest, and dignified work to which they had committed their lives.

Recently the background rumble of historical and epistemological debate has swelled to a deafening roar. A whole series of powerful individuals and movements has challenged the meaning and validity of the work of historians far more deeply than Beard and Becker ever dreamed of doing. It has been impressively argued that historical truth is not only unattainable but meaningless as a concept, that historians and other writers are always engaged in a struggle for class power whether they know it or not, even that words have no meaning or reference beyond themselves. In my last years of teaching, a few of the brightest graduate students I taught were devoted to Foucault and aware, from their English courses, of Derrida. More and more, young historians were fighting battles for and against the new theoretical challenges in meetings, journals, and books.[3]

Of course, there were and are many able and intelligent historians who care for none of these things. This had been true in the age of Beard and Becker. But this time, I have the impression that some of those who feel most deeply threatened are among the most sensitive and intelligent, and those most aware of arguments outside the historical profession, among philosophers and literary critics. Specialists in intellectual history are especially likely to feel challenged. What some of them are suffering from is no trivial malaise; it is a special form of the fear of meaninglessness, an ancient enemy that has long ravaged the days and nights of the young and gifted.

It is worth noticing, however, that logically or not, few give up writing history because of this sort of challenge. How is this possible? One might equally well ask how it is possible for people to go on living when they can no longer coherently explain the meaning of life. Yet there have never been many suicides because of philosophical *Angst* alone—no doubt some, but not many. I do not mean at all to belittle these very real challenges. Nor do I mean to get into the hard work of refuting the skeptics—I am not sure that they can be refuted. The vogue of Foucault and Derrida will pass—perhaps in the most sophisticated circles this is already happening. If so, their places will surely be taken by thinkers who are equally disturbing to traditional historical thought.

Publishing a book of historical essays at such a time of profound historical debate, I find that "a decent respect to the opinion of mankind" (or rather that tiny fragment of it that is concerned about these matters) requires that I set forth not my theories but my practicing assumptions. Because of my training, the only way I know how to begin this task is to try to explain, as clearly as I am able, how these assumptions grew.

Of the events and tendencies that have formed my attitudes toward historical writing, I must begin with the escapist romanticism of a bookish childhood, which led me to the pleasures of imagining another time and place. I suspect that most historians start this way, though few admit it. Perhaps some get entirely over it; I certainly have not.

In my twenties and thirties this tendency was tempered by another, opposite and equally powerful, my long involvement with 1930s-style Marxism. I tried hard to see history as one long process, determined by class struggle and bound to eventuate in a classless society. Like many others, and later than some, I abandoned this view in a painful process of disillusion in the 1950s. What did it leave as residues that have affected my historical work? Perhaps, on the positive side, some feeling for the place of power and interest in all history. This was, however, balanced by a revulsion against simplification and monocausal explanations. These had certainly pervaded Marxist history written in America, whether or not Marx is to be blamed for this fact.

While my romantic and Marxist inclinations were both fully operative, both were checked and challenged by my encounter with my first real pro, Professor Arthur M. Schlesinger (Sr.), who became my thesis supervisor at Harvard. I respected and liked Mr. Schlesinger, but eventually I rejected many of his precepts. He was a holdout for objective truth and the detached observer, and in this period of his life saw Beard in particular as something of a menace. In actual fact, every word Schlesinger ever wrote voted for Jefferson, Jackson, and Franklin Roosevelt. He presented American history as broadening democracy, gradually overcoming obstacles. After I overcame some of my awe, I actually told him once that his *Rise of the City* seemed to me a bit too optimistic. He agreed that perhaps it was. It was Schlesinger's greatest strength as a graduate teacher that he never demanded that his students either agree with him or work on his kind of subject.

Almost the only thing A. M. Schlesinger *did* demand and enforce was that his students refrain from drawing conclusions or even formulating precise questions before they had immersed themselves, exhaustingly if not ex-

haustively, in the sources. I have never gotten over thinking that such immersion is a *sine qua non* of good history.
The long hours in the library are more than mere drudgery, they provide the only nourishment for the historical
imagination. To me, the smell of the sources, the product
of long exposure to the language and symbols as well
as the ideas of the past, gives history most of its aesthetic appeal. I think it is possible to tell within the first
few pages of a historical work whether it has this quality
or not.

Once again, in this crazily dialectical process, I was
jarred, immensely impressed, and pushed in an opposite
direction by Perry Miller. It is my impression that Schlesinger and Miller got along quite well because they were
such opposites: they did not talk the same language
enough to argue with each other. Schlesinger's opponent
was Beard; Miller's, F. O. Matthiessen, who was, like
Miller, a member of the Harvard English Department
and, more than Miller, a political radical. As against
Schlesinger, who assumed, rather than arguing, that
ideas were part of a continuum that included everything
from street railways to costumes or popular literature,
Miller made past idea-systems not only an independent
subject of study, but just about the only really interesting
part of history. Past idea systems needed not just to be
summarized by historians but to be analyzed, felt, almost
lived—though not, of course, believed. As a part of this
approach, Miller insisted that religious ideas, central to
the Puritans (who engaged most of his energies) and also
to their heirs from Jonathan Edwards to Ralph Waldo
Emerson, must be taken most seriously of all by those
who want to understand the New England mind.
Though I did not realize it then, I *had* a New England
mind, derived from my New England father, a serious
post-Calvinist seeker with whom my relation was as difficult as it was important.[4]

A further powerful influence in this direction was Reinhold Niebuhr, whose work I first seriously encountered in my early teaching career.[5] Immediately on reading him, I was powerfully attracted by what I took to be his central message, the thoroughly post-Calvinist dictum, stated in a way that seemed adaptable even to secular purposes, that one cannot win but has to try. I think that the Niebuhrian conviction that human beings have to seek the truth but will never really find it has immediately and powerfully affected my attitude to all sorts of problems, including those of writing history. Indeed, the effect was so strong that I realize that I must have been thinking along these lines long before reading Niebuhr. Well before being exposed to recent critics, I had taken for granted that words never quite reflect prior realities. One can never reach the truth, but one goes on trying to get a little closer.

At about the same time, strenuously engaged in teaching American intellectual history, I found that of all the past thinkers I read and talked about year after year, the one who spoke to me the most forcefully was William James. One side of this often baffling thinker offers immense help and comfort to those who find that they have to get along without granitic certainties, and must rather bet their lives on the unfinished, the shifting, the provisional.

This general tendency to accept the need of taking chances was reinforced by my encounter with the student revolt at Berkeley in the 1960s, a movement or set of movements to which I found myself at first sympathetic, later opposed. One consequence of this engrossing and disturbing experience was that the students forced me to abandon the intellectual history copout. About each subject that came up, sixties students asked me what I personally thought and felt. Like others, I had been in the habit of answering that this was not what we were studying; we were trying to achieve a neutral understanding of what certain people, now dead, had thought and felt in their time. Reluctantly but permanently, I decided that this answer and this dichotomy were no good—you cannot understand the past except through your own present feelings and attitudes. I learned this fact, I believe, far more by trial and error than by reading the many thinkers who proclaim its truth.

Another important influence on my thinking and my work, all the way from graduate school experience until his death in 1987, was Henry Nash Smith. In our frequent discussions, Smith's sophisticated skepticism tempered my romantic susceptibilities and brought into question my religious experiments in a very useful way. Smith had formed many of his convictions in the skeptical twenties, by a prodigious and entirely individual study of anthropologists, philosophers, and critics.[6] When I first knew him at Harvard, he had long taken for granted the inadequacy of nineteenth-century positivism and the "scientific history" that still reflected its assumptions. On the same sort of skeptical grounds, Smith largely resisted the thirties vogue of simple historical materialism.

All these major influences, and doubtless many others of which I am not aware, have shaped my response to recent historical argument. With them in mind, I should like briefly to state my working position on a few of the questions now being intensely discussed. Some of these questions deal with the legitimacy of various kinds of history. To me, the meaning of history and the method of getting at it are both interesting subjects for discussion, but what constitutes the proper subject matter of history is not. Anything that historians perceive to have existed in the past is a legitimate subject. History is enriched when people discover new subjects for investigation. It is also enriched by those who look at thoroughly traditional subjects in new ways.

When I began teaching and writing, many questioned the legitimacy of intellectual history. Of course some still do, but now a question more often argued is that of the autonomy of intellectual history. Here I think that in some of my earlier work I have, through my own fault, been misunderstood. I have repeatedly argued that the history of what people thought and felt in the past (to me the two are not separable) is as legitimate and important a topic as any other division of history. This was in reaction to the easy assumption that all history, including the history of ideas, is easily explicable in terms of economic interests and that what is important is mainly political results. Exactly this is no longer said by sophisticated historians, but it is still sometimes an unspoken assumption.

Some of my statements about this matter have probably been too defensive. I have certainly never have meant to imply either that intellectual history is superior to other kinds of history or that it is separable from them. Thinking is done by people, and people cannot be cut into segments without being killed. When historians of thought or culture (to me the term "intellectual historians" has a slightly snobbish ring) talk only to each other, they run the risk of a sort of collective solipsism. One cannot write a really *historical* account of the thought of, for instance, William James, without having in mind the political, social, economic, scientific, and even diplomatic history of James's time. Yet even a small and technical part of James's philosophy is a perfectly legitimate subject for truly historical treatment, and the various kinds of historical "background" need not be inappropriately dragged into the foreground.

Within intellectual history there has been a certain amount of argument about whether the genre includes popular as well as high-level, fully developed ideas. Here again the answer is easy: the boundaries of specialism do not matter except perhaps to those administering departments, and no level of thought need be excluded. One may choose to deal only with professional philosophers, or only with large popular movements. All that is important here is that one should be conscious of the approximate size of the segment one is dealing with (often a very tricky business) and of the position of this segment in relation to those excluded from it.

Being free to choose, I have usually chosen to deal with the thought of the articulate spokesmen of the dominant culture, and I have given a great deal of time and effort to trying to find out who these were. (Here, some Marxist historians have useful things to say.) Obviously, in the United States, these spokesmen have been members of the middle class, again a term notoriously difficult to define. I have tried very hard to find ways to tell who in a given period were vested with the indefinable but widely recognized authority of cultural spokesmen. Through the statements of these men or women, I have tried to get at the important things that were so obvious and generally agreed on that they had to be articulated only in times of crisis. Sometimes what is not said is quite as revealing as what is said.

A related question is that of the canon. Whether a generally recognized group of major writers is the proper subject of study has legitimately exercised literary historians. For historians, the question of a canon is also a legitimate subject of argument. It seems to me indisputable that canons have always existed and that they change over time. Among the questions that historians should think about are how canons come into

existence, how they change, why some writers or thinkers are inside the walls and some outside, and how these
walls are defended and attacked.

Finally, I must get to the most difficult question.
Should one try to enter imaginatively into the mind of
the past or, recognizing that this is not entirely possible,
should one ask of the past the questions most important
here and now, to writer and to reader, to you and to
me. I have always assumed that one should try to do
both. I used to tell students they should first study the
past in its own terms and then ask their own questions
about it. I now realize that it is not possible to separate
these two operations. During all one's research, one tries
to learn from the sources what people really cared about
then, and this is bound to have some bearing on what
questions one would like most to ask the some sources
now. Unlike social scientists, historians do not characteristically approach their subjects with a list of problems
already formulated. The questions, the answers, the definition of the subject, the organization of the project
change all the time, during the research and the writing.
This is what makes writing history arduous, and this is
what gives history much of its vitality.

And of course we must realize, whether we accept or
reject the most challenging contemporary critics, that
whatever our purpose or method we can never really
get at the past. As Beard and Becker pointed out in their
day, historians cannot escape the assumptions and prejudices of their own time, nor can they escape their own
personal histories and effects of these on their styles and
emotions. If it were possible for historians to eliminate
their personalities and opinions, the resulting work
would be uninteresting and unreadable.

Reviewers sometimes say that certain historians or certain points of view are dated. It occurs to me that the

historians that last the longest are sometimes the most dated. Reading Gibbon, we see the late Roman Empire through the eyes of an eighteenth-century skeptic. Reading Leslie Stephen, we see British eighteenth-century thought through the eyes of a Victorian agnostic. Reading Henry Adams's *History,* we see the administrations of Jefferson and his successor through the eyes of an Adams. Yet none of these historians was a superficial presentist; all spent long hours listening to what the past had to say. All, however, knew that they were dealing with the past in terms of their own deepest loyalties.

Finally, I am led by whatever experience I have had to agree with Beard that history depends on an act of faith. Much more than he realized, it depends on many acts of faith constantly made. Faith that the past exists. That we can achieve some meaningful relation with it. That words have some meaning. That a usable pattern will emerge from one's reading and note-taking. That this pattern will have meaning to some people beside oneself.

What is the alternative to such acts of faith? Are we to insist that our students, before they start writing, read a great deal of recent and contemporary philosophy and arrive at clear conclusions about the questions raised? This might produce more philosophers, but it would stop cold the production of historians. Or are we to prohibit the reading of, say, Foucault until one has written at least an M.A. thesis? Perhaps the final act of faith is faith in our students and successors, that is, in the survival of history itself. Such acts of faith have always been necessary; the achievement of modern criticism has been to make the necessity obvious.

I Allegiances

1

Religion and American Intellectual History, 1945–1985: Reflections on an Uneasy Relationship

In 1986 I was asked to present a paper on this topic at a conference at the Smithsonian Institution. The topic had been so central in my teaching and thinking that I found I could not approach it in an impersonal mode. This essay, therefore, like the Introduction that precedes it, is directly autobiographical. The two pieces discuss some of the same persons and episodes, but the emphasis and purpose of each are obviously quite different. The other two essays in this section also deal with influences on my thinking and writing, and there are some autobiographical elements in other essays in this volume. Perhaps the addiction to reminiscence is the consequence of working for several years on a book about my childhood and youth. In any case, as one gets old, for better or worse present thinking becomes inseparable from reflecting on past experience.

This essay was first published in Michael J. Lacey, ed., Religion and Twentieth-Century American Intellectual

Life (Cambridge, Mass., 1989), and is reprinted by permission of the Woodrow Wilson International Center for Scholars.

In the late thirties, when I was in graduate school, the progressive interpretation of American history had the allegiance of nearly everybody I knew. Part of the progressive ideology was the assumption that religion was and must be declining. Democracy and progress were closely associated with the liberation of mankind from superstition. Religion was dependent on a series of dogmas and legends that no serious intellectual could entertain. This set of views, proclaimed with passion in the late eighteenth century and gathering strength through the first half of the nineteenth, had often been challenged. Yet for many these assumptions were deeply taken for granted, lodged in the unconscious, where assumptions are hardest to dislodge.

So strong, in fact, was this progressive and secular view of history that Auschwitz and Hiroshima had only damaged, not destroyed it. In the postwar years, the disillusion of most American intellectuals with the Soviet Union, the self-proclaimed heartland of progress and bastion of secularity, did rather more damage. Yet the progressive view of history succumbed only very slowly. For many American intellectuals in the complacent fifties, disillusion with foreign ideologies rather reinforced their belief in the rise of American civilization.

In 1947 I got a job at Scripps College, and inherited a course called "American Social and Political Ideas." Five years later, in 1952, I was invited to join the history department at the University of California in Berkeley, with the specific assignment of introducing a brand-new course to be called American Intellectual History. To me, no assignment could have been more gratifying and challenging, than this, and for the rest of the fifties I spent most of my time developing and improving this course. (In Berkeley, the fifties lasted until the Fall of 1964.) This was, for many reasons, a time of very high academic morale, and nowhere more than at Berkeley.

I had worked at Harvard with Arthur M. Schlesinger. I liked and respected Professor Schlesinger but wanted to break sharply with his way of teaching American social and intellectual history together. If one had to move rapidly between a short summary of Emerson or Thoreau and a description of the effects of the invention of the detachable collar, it seemed to me that critical examination of either kind of phenomenon was impossible. I tried therefore to organize a course in which the foreground was clearly and exclusively ideas, the background society. The way I constructed this course was to choose a set of sources for the students to read and for us to discuss. I had already learned at Scripps how quickly intellectual history could pall if undergraduates read many monographs. Sources were the subject itself, and the style, tone, and passion as important as what was said.

I am afraid my choice of source assignments was a bit arbitrary, and it was of course greatly affected by what was available in the bookstores then—right at the beginning of the paperback revolution. Of course I started with the New England Puritans. This choice was not only congenial, it was inevitable. I had, after all, learned about the Puritans from Perry Miller, who had discovered— some critics have almost said invented—them. Equally obviously, it was necessary to spend some time with the great political intellectuals of the Enlightenment. A little later, I clearly had to deal with the Transcendentalists, proclaimed—once again by Perry Miller—as the patron saints of all American intellectual rebels. After that things got more complicated, but one could hardly leave out the pragmatic philosophers, so often said by themselves and others to be quintessentially American. Beyond these it seemed right to pay my respects to recent American literature and social science.

These were all the ideas of respectable intellectuals. But I had my own democratic allegiances, and I knew that there were large numbers of people in the country who were interesting and articulate and yet not concerned full-time with the ideas of Edwards or Emerson or James. So the course had to find a place for another range of topics, for the less systematic ideas of Jacksonian Democrats, Southern nationalists, abolitionists, and later those of Populists, progressives, socialists, isolationists, one-worlders.

There is no doubt that I was combining apples and oranges with not a few pears. Every now and then a bright graduate student who was auditing the course would politely suggest that it was an epistemological jungle. I suspected that this might be correct, but for a while it did not bother me a lot. The excitement of creating the course was too heady. Not all undergraduates liked it; some decided it was not for them about halfway through my—or really, Perry Miller's—treatment of the tension between Arminianism and antinomianism. But those who stayed were often enthusiastic. After all, in their reading they were coming into direct contact with some pretty exciting people. A solid handful of excellent graduate students found topics for research in my course and seminars. Their close and intense reexaminations of many important topics gradually refined and improved my lectures. Intellectual history was not, of course, accepted by all members of the history department. Some of my senior colleagues made occasional slighting remarks about the difficulty of nailing jelly to the wall. But nobody was persecuted; there was just enough disapproval to give teachers and students working in American intellectual history the feeling of being a daring minority. Intellectual history was just enough out to be in, and by the end of the fifties it was unquestionably in.

From time to time a student would ask me why we were spending so much time on *religion*. It was easy to argue that this topic had been all-important in the seventeenth century. After that, since the question had not been settled by Perry Miller, my answers became more complicated. I had, however, begun to encounter Paul Tillich, who seemed to define religion so as to mean—almost—anything that was really important to anybody.

Far more important to me (as to many in these years) was Tillich's colleague Reinhold Niebuhr. *The Irony of American History* was published in 1952, the year I arrived in Berkeley. Here was a godsend for the end of my course in intellectual history. Here was an unquestionably serious thinker to balance Jonathan Edwards near the beginning. He was talking about the whole range of American culture, and also about the most pressing problems of the moment: war, peace, the bomb, relations with the Soviet Union. Moreover, the view he was expressing was the one toward which I, like many of my colleagues, had been slowly moving—a point of view balanced between the old radicalism and the new, somewhat reluctant patriotism. Above all, Niebuhr seemed to be looking at these matters as nearly as possible *sub specie aeternitatis*. He was telling us we could not make the right political decisions if our starting point was political. Going through the *Irony* year after year, and reading Niebuhr's other works, I was brought to the question: if politics is not primary, what is? (I was temperamentally unable to answer, "Nothing.")

This was at least part of the transition from an interest in religious history to an interest in religion itself. These were the years of the much-discussed revival of interest in religion. The churches around the campus were filling up and so were their treasuries. If on the campus we dismissed most of the public religiosity of the Eisenhower era, there were still the intellectual theologians. Tillich's visit to Berkeley in this period was a public triumph. In an overflow meeting in the gym he proclaimed that the war between science and religion was over: scientists and theologians were simply not talking about the same subject. Another visitor was Billy Graham, who spoke in the Greek Theater. The first part of his talk was a convincing and well-informed discussion of the despair of modern culture. This far, the large crowd went with him. When he started to talk about where one could turn for help in this situation he probably lost most of his audience.

There were of course many who opposed the revival and probably many more who knew nothing of it. Only a few joined churches. The group of academics most characteristic of the period were those characterized with great acuteness by Sydney Ahlstrom as "curious about religion."[1] I belonged in this category. In my teaching in the 1950s I made use of Richard Niebuhr's two books on American religion. In one, *The Social Sources of Denominationalism* (1929), Niebuhr applied to American religion a straight Weberian social science analysis. In the second, *The Kingdom of God in America* (1937), he somewhat repudiated his earlier approach. If one wants to understand religious history, he now told us, one must concern himself not just with social causes and results of religious movements but with the actual intellectual and still more the emotional content of faith: not just with the sociological banks, but with the living stream that flowed between them. In the 1950s, newly "interested in religion," I found this metaphor extremely powerful. It asked us to treat religion in just the way I was trying to treat all the ideas I talked about in my class.

Outside the universities, sometimes as at Berkeley almost across the street, were the seminaries. In this period of revival some seminary historians were feeling their oats and calling for a church history entirely free of secular influence. This meant a sharp separation from university historians. A few excellent scholars were able to transcend this division. From the seminary side, Sidney Mead was a biting critic of complacency. Among university historians, Sidney Ahlstrom, William Hutchison, and Timothy Smith were for different reasons acceptable on both sides of this particular divide.

It was against this background that I wrote and, after some years of thought and revision, submitted to *The American Historical Review* an essay called "The Recovery of American Religious History."[2] In this essay I talked about a coming together of various tendencies in social history, literary history, and intellectual history under the twin influences of religious revival and theological renewal. The result was, I said, a restoration of the historic and vitalizing American argument between religious and secular interpretations of the American past.

This article was, I think, a satisfactory statement of the way things looked to me then. The only trouble was that it was published in 1964, exactly when all the conditions I had talked about in the article were coming to an abrupt and dramatic end. Both religious revival and theological renewal suddenly slowed down. Neo-orthodoxy in general and Reinhold Niebuhr in particular underwent harsh attack. Niebuhr was rejected by the excited optimists of the early sixties as a merchant of gloom. For a very brief period his teachings seemed to be replaced by the cosmic optimism of Harvey Cox, who pinned his religious hopes on, of all things, the American city. Later, in the less euphoric late sixties, Niebuhr was attacked as a Cold Warrior. The churches, dwindling somewhat in numbers and funds, became embroiled, sometimes heroically, in the Civil Rights movement and later in the opposition to the Vietnam War.

Sweating out the sixties at any major American campus was an experience never to be forgotten. Not only did we live though brief periods of the actual breakdown of social order; more important, the *intellectual* order of the fifties was shattered beyond repair. Detachment became copout, intellectuality, elitism, tolerance, repressive. The more we tried to understand and analyze the movement of the young the more it changed its form in our grasp. I remember once when I was threatened with disruption of my class unless I would allow some political announcements to be made at the beginning of it. "Do you think," I was asked, "that American intellectual history, of all irrelevant subjects, is more important than justice for the Third World?" Reduced to intellectual rock-bottom, I answered, "Right here, in 151 Dwinelle Hall at three o'clock, it is." That time I got away with it and the class went on.

In the sixties, though the popular revival came to an end, the intellectual interest in religion did not. In my class I found it very easy to explain what antinomianism was—it was all around us. Once I was concluding a lecture on Transcendentalism and remarked that the movement really couldn't have lasted; it had no program but a change of heart. A student told me that this was typical academic blindness; ideas just like those I had been discussing were all around us on the campus. Robert Bellah, who moved in 1967 from what he called "the magisterial certainty of Harvard" to the "wide-open chaos of Berkeley" because he found the latter more congenial, was one of the first to present the contemporary student movement, with approval, as a religious revival.[3] The more I thought about this the more completely persuasive I found it. Like the many religious revivals of the American past, the movement was unpredictable; like the spirit, it blew where it would. Like the other revivals, it was at its height impossible to resist or control; like them, it was soon over, leaving different kinds of effects on different kinds of people.

Meantime the historians who had come to maturity in the fifties were attacked from quite another quarter. Professor John Higham, a rigorous moralist who was anything but an ally of the young rebels, seemed in part to echo their criticisms in a series of powerful and influential essays on what he called consensus history. According to Higham, historians reacting against the progressive synthesis had produced "a bland history, in which conflict was muted, in which the classic issues of social justice were underplayed, in which the elements of spontaneity, effervescence, and violence in American life got little sympathy or attention."[4] Higham's picture was largely accurate and his criticism was taken to heart; it was part of the period's shaking of academic complacency. On behalf of those criticized as consensus historians, I would like to make only two points. First, it is one thing to say that in American history—as opposed, for instance, to French or Russian history—consensus has indeed prevailed; quite another to say that this fact makes America superior. Second, the historians who had in the age of Niebuhr abandoned the tradition of Beard and Parrington, with its clear dichotomies between progressive and conservative, had done so reluctantly, as they gradually found this progressive synthesis unworkable.

One minor—to some of us not so minor—effect of the major upheaval of the sixties was to make intellectual history unfashionable. This loss of prestige was continued in the seventies with the many triumphs of the new social history. Using a whole battery of exciting new techniques, the new social historians were finding ways to learn about people in the past things they had never known about themselves. Ideas consciously held and articulated became correspondingly less interesting. This was no doubt a perfectly legitimate, though not an inevitable choice. The other part of the attack was less convincing; the argument that an interest in intellectual history was somehow elitist, a view that seemed to imply that ordinary people don't have ideas, opinions, or ideologies.

The prestigious new social historians were, however, intensely interested in the history of religion, with certain strict provisos. It must be popular religion, preferably heretical, anti-establishment religion. What was interesting was not developed theologies or successful institutions, but rather the practices, however strange and painful, of the Cathari, the shepherds of the Pyrenees, or the decidedly eccentric cosmology of an Italian miller victimized by the Inquisition, or the cults and sorceries practiced by anonymous villagers.

Part of the reason for these particular negative and positive choices was that this new social history spread from Paris. In continental Europe, and especially in France, attitudes toward religion were until very recently inseparably connected with political loyalties going all the way back to the great Revolution. On one side were the Republic—the Enlightenment, democracy, and, for many, socialism. Against these were ranged the church and the other forces of reaction. The power of this traditional division was made clear to me at a series of international conferences I attended. At a meeting on the Enlightenment held at Yale in 1975, a brave French professor, Georges Gusdorf, questioned the dominant organization of French eighteenth-century religious history. This then tended to move from the anti-clericalism of the Enlightenment toward a widening and deepening rejection of religion, culminating in the official revolutionary de-Christianization promoted by Robespierre. Gusdorf suggested that the story was really a lot more complicated than that, that the conventional French view ignored large groups of passionately religious people. This produced two hours of impassioned oratory in which Gusdorf was accused of treason to the memory of the *Lumières*.

For another meeting, in Poland, I was asked to give a paper on the Enlightenment in America. In passing, I made a point, to me obvious, that evangelical Protestantism was the usual religion of the people, while religious liberalism was usually associated with the upper middle class. I found that some people in my European audience found this statement not so much wrong as incomprehensible. Religion was associated with authority; the people were revolting against authority and therefore against religion. Whether or not this is a tenable synthesis of modern European religious history, it will certainly not work for America. We have learned a great deal from recent European historians; there are some lessons we should reject.

In addition to the challenge from European and American social history, intellectual historians were strongly affected by American social scientists, and religious historians were especially influenced by anthropologists and sociologists of religion. Among the latter were some committed Christians like Peter Berger and Robert Bellah, whose prestige helped to widen the choices available. Berger in particular told us that culture was in part constitutive of social reality, which gave useful ammunition against social historians who strongly implied the opposite. Unquestionably the most influential figure, however, was Clifford Geertz—literate, elegant, catholic in sympathies, empathetic but supremely detached. To Geertz, religion was an all-important set of symbols, indispensable for giving meaning and legitimacy to a culture.

In political science, brilliant students of the history of political theory—Quentin Skinner, John Dunn, John Pocock—were talking about the history of speech, of discourse, of changing paradigms. All this seemed to legitimate some kinds of intellectual history.

Many of these tendencies were made manifest in the 1977 Wingspread conference on American intellectual history.[5] There an extremely talented group of young intellectual historians showed themselves on the defensive toward the new social history and profoundly appreciative of legitimation by social and political scientists. The devotion and intelligence of this group of young scholars seemed to me to make their sometimes defensive and apologetic tone highly inappropriate.

The much-discussed decline of intellectual history in this period was not a decline in the quality of the books written or the courses taught. It was a decline in professional prestige and esteem, and this was reflected, concretely and damagingly, in changes in curriculum and the loss of job opportunities. I would like at this point to state my respect and admiration for the many young historians then entering the field, who insisted on doing the kind of history they believed in, often at truly heroic cost.

On the other hand, religious history continued to gain in this period in vitality, diversity, and excellence, though it was not the religious history of Perry Miller and his followers or of the traditional church historians.

Let me finally (and briefly) try to say how things are now with these two topics, in the mid–1980s. First, intellectual history has recovered some of its lost prestige. One can see this in the most concrete terms: there are a few more positions advertised. Perhaps this partial recovery is related to the widespread, or at least much-articulated, concern for the humanities in general. People may have realized that while there is an excellent case for exposing students to other cultures, there is no good reason to keep them ignorant of their own. There is no liberation in *not* having read Edwards and Emerson and James.

To some degree, I think, intellectual history has been educated by its vicissitudes. There is less tendency to separate it from social history—the separation was always temporary and tactical and may have been unwise. There are fewer books tracing the influence of one book on another. There is less tendency to talk about the Puritan mind, the Southern mind, the American mind, in terms of only the few most accessible sources.

Second, I think American *religious* history may be better and more esteemed than ever before. There is some recognition that it combines intellectual history, social history, and the anthropological study of rituals and symbols. Among general American historians, some topics in religion have reached center stage. Puritanism remains there, and the discussion of it is still likely to center on where Perry Miller was wrong. This is the greatest compliment a later period can pay to a great historian. (When I was in graduate school all historiographical discussion began with the question where Frederick Jackson Turner was wrong.) Moving forward into the nineteenth century, revivalism is almost as much a standard topic as Puritanism. Few historians of antislavery, whatever their ideological preferences, would now leave out the massive influence of evangelical Protestantism.

When one gets to later periods, recognition of the importance of religious history is more sporadic. At a recent meeting one of the very best intellectual historians in the country announced, a little in the tone of a person who has had a special revelation and cannot quite believe it, that in dealing with late nineteenth-century social reform one really must take social Christianity seriously.

How about religion itself? I was very surprised to see a recent survey cited in the *New York Review of Books* saying that 64 percent of all faculty members consider themselves "deeply" or "moderately" religious, and 48 percent attend services once a month or more.[6] This must include denominational colleges; it certainly would not describe the institutions I know well.

In a recent committee meeting in Berkeley a very eminent biochemist told me that he did not see how any research dealing with religion could be significant or interesting. I think that this forthright and robust sort of statement has become much more rare than it used to be. Certainly among historians it is now generally regarded as crude to be rude in talking about religion. It is still much easier to be respectful when talking about times past. The idea that science, somehow in alliance with broadening democracy, has made religion impossible dies very hard. In discussing the present, there is a tendency among academics to fear Fundamentalism, and sometimes to identify all evangelical Protestantism with the political Far Right. In a recent review, David Brion Davis, a historian I admire, characterized the present as "a time when American culture is ominously divided between fundamentalists and secular humanists."[7] That seems to be what Fundamentalists themselves think. Most of the sound and fury does indeed come from these two camps, but there are still millions of Americans and even quite a few academic intellectuals who belong in neither of them.

And now I come to the very last and most personal part of my talk. I would like to suggest a few planks for a platform on which historians dealing with American religion might be able to come together.

First, nobody questions openly, and I think few question privately, that ordinary standards of scholarly accuracy must apply to sacred subjects. This has always been necessary in a country that does not agree on what is sacred. If there are any exceptions to this rule—and there should not be—they probably apply to subjects that are sacred to the civil religion rather than to the religions of the churches.

Second, the idea is long dead that one needs to belong to a certain persuasion to write well about it. This was first courageously demonstrated in 1958 by Robert Cross, a Protestant writing one of the best books on the history of American Catholicism. It is easy to think of a Catholic doing excellent work on Mormonism, an Episcopalian dealing sympathetically with Boston Unitarianism, a Mormon writing with insight about New England Calvinism. It is impossible to say how many of the best books in religious history are written by agnostics; certainly many of them, possibly most.

But that is not quite all I want to say. My third plank is clearly more controversial. To write excellent religious history, I believe, one must have something like religious sensibility or imagination. Obviously, one does not have to be a believer. It is possible to write well about something one totally disbelieves, fears, or hates. But it is really not possible to write excellent history about something one dismisses, however tacitly, as unimportant. Somehow one's definition of reality must be broad enough to include the religious stream as well as the sociological banks between which it flows.

2

The Rough Road to *Virgin Land*

When I was asked to contribute to a book of essays in honor of Henry Nash Smith, my friend for more than forty years, I asked if I could contribute, instead of a scholarly article, a brief study of Henry Smith's early life. The editor cordially agreed to this request. My reasons for wanting to do this were several. First was gratitude; ever since graduate school Henry Smith had been the second reader (after my wife) of almost everything I wrote. I had profited immensely from his special combination of understanding support and cool criticism, all the more because many of his ideas were quite different from my own. Second, I had been convinced in the course of many conversations that Smith's early experiences were both interesting in themselves and important for the full understanding of his work. I decided my stopping point would be the publication of Virgin Land, *the book that even its severest critics agree gave a pattern to the new field of American Studies, for since that book's publication Smith's career is well known.*

I wrote this sketch with the complete and generous cooperation of its subject. It is based mainly on interviews, conducted in the Fall of 1984, less than two years before Henry Smith's death. The interviews were supplemented by reading documents that Henry lent me, and by some research of my own. Though I tried in writing the sketch to present primarily Henry Smith's own view of his early life, the occasional interpretive and critical comments are my own. When he read the piece, he approved it as an accurate account of the facts and of his own statements without commenting on my interpretive remarks.

This essay has been published in American Literature, Culture, and Ideology: Essays in Memory of Henry Nash Smith *(ed. Beverly Voloshin, New York, 1989) and is reprinted by permission of Peter Lang Publishing, Inc.*

Henry Nash Smith was born in Dallas, Texas, in 1906. While he was growing up there, Dallas was not yet the Big D, with big art, big music, big religion, and big politics, all paid for by big oil. It was a town of under 50,000 people, just beginning a period of fast growth. Incorporated in 1856, Dallas got a sudden influx of discouraged former Confederates from the Southeast, just at the end of the war. Modest prosperity got under way in 1872, when the town, by a strenuous campaign a little like that described in Mark Twain's *The Gilded Age,* managed to become the crossing point of two railroads.

The amenities of city life were much slower getting started in Dallas than in many American cities. By the time of Henry Smith's childhood there were good hotels, ladies' literary societies, a large Methodist bookstore said to be much less sectarian in its offerings than most such establishments, and a public library well below national standards for cities the size of Dallas. Neiman-Marcus got its modest beginning in 1907; Southern Methodist University was to open its doors only in 1915.

Around Dallas the country is flat and the trees few and scrubby. There are no forests, mountains, or natural lakes for a very long way. When Henry Smith first encountered literary raptures about nature, he says, he could not understand what the poets were talking about. Before air conditioning, the long hot summers were an endurance test. In winter the temperature could drop forty degrees in a day and windstorms called "blue northers" were common. Tornadoes, floods, and droughts were by no means unknown.

Dallas inherited the traditions of both West and South. Before the boom in cotton shipping it had been a cow town like its rival Fort Worth, and oldtimers could tell stories of bandits and rustlers. In 1902 the city had enthusiastically welcomed the annual reunion of the Confederate Veterans. Henry Smith remembered reading about one local lynching. The schools were segregated three ways—for whites, blacks, and Mexicans. Among the whites only a few were very rich, and people who put on airs were distinctly unpopular. Most people were polite, and many were good at telling stories.

Henry's father, of Kentucky origins, was an accountant. He had learned his business not in school, but through long practice. Recently, Texas had set up examinations for CPA's, but reputable citizens already practicing had been exempted from such requirements, "grandfathered in," in the local phrase. In a very common American pattern, Henry remembered his father as absolutely upright and somewhat severe, by no means given to expressing his emotions. His mother, whose family came from Alabama and Mississippi, had been a beauty and coquette in her youth and was affectionate and lively with Henry, his younger brother, and his sister. Mrs. Smith's mother, Mrs. Nash, remembered the Confederate army marching home, tired and lousy. When Henry, in Dallas, brought home a schoolbook with a picture of two great presidents, Washington and Lincoln, Mrs. Nash was outraged. Lincoln was a vulgar bar-

barian; Washington, together with Lee, the pattern of a Virginia gentleman.

In back of the house, and most houses, was a cabin for the black servant, who helped with the cooking and housework. Henry remembered her washing clothes outdoors in a big iron pot. Since insubordination was unthinkable, the family's relations with her were relaxed and friendly. She got a nice present at Christmas, and went when necessary to the same doctor as the rest of the family.

Next door, in a similar house with a similar servant's cabin out back, lived Henry's father's sister and her husband, Aunt Maud and Uncle Randolph. I was very surprised to learn that Uncle Randolph was a graduate of Harvard College and Law School and asked Henry if that did not convey considerable social prestige. He insisted that this was not the case. Uncle Randolph, who owned two farms near Denton, Texas, did nothing but sit on the porch all day. Moreover, he seldom wore a coat and tie. Such lazy and sloppy ways were not approved in Dallas, and Henry's father joined in the disapproval. With Uncle Randolph and Aunt Maud lived Henry's paternal grandfather, whom Henry remembered as an imposing bearded man who was assistant cashier in a bank. His only duties, Henry believed, were to sit at a desk near the door looking dignified and affable and greeting customers. Uncle Randolph's son, also Randolph, was Henry's age and naturally became his companion and rival. Sometimes Uncle Randolph took the two boys shooting quail, near Denton. This was regarded as a correct manly pursuit, but Henry remembered it as boring. The two next-door families took turns inviting each other for Christmas and Thanksgiving dinner, but this is almost the only entertaining Henry remembers. His family in the two houses was in childhood the only society he knew.

Henry told me at first that he did not remember seeing anybody read a book in either house. Later he remembered that his mother, who belonged to a ladies' literary club, occasionally read popular romances. His father read the *Saturday Evening Post* and the *Literary Digest;* his mother the *Ladies' Home Journal.* Far more important to Henry, however, was the fact that Uncle Randolph owned a set of the Harvard classics, President Eliot's famous five-foot shelf. This collection purported to include all the most important books in all fields of learning. Its salesmen claimed that fifteen minutes a day with the five-foot shelf would make anybody a cultivated person. Henry attacked the collection with great interest. One of his favorites was Darwin's *Voyage of the Beagle,* and he also remembered reading Plato's *Republic* and Bacon's *Advancement of Learning.* Moving on from the five-foot shelf to the Dallas Public Library, by his teens he had read a good deal of Kipling and some Stevenson and Mark Twain. (At first he preferred *Tom Sawyer,* but by high school days delighted in *Huckleberry Finn.*) He read *Les Miserables* and *Don Quixote* in translation, and even plowed through Creasy's *Fifteen Decisive Battles of the World.* Then and later, Henry Smith's taste in reading has been serious. As a boy he sampled only a few of his mother's historical novels. He did not read "boys' books" like the action-filled tales of G. A. Henty, and he has never developed an addiction to detective stories. He was never at all attracted to romances of the Lost Cause or stories of the Wild West. Almost his only reading of subliterature came much later, and was undertaken for the purpose of professional analysis.

Like most citizens of Dallas, Henry's parents were deeply involved with religion. They were members of the Disciples of Christ, the church founded in the early nineteenth century by Thomas and Alexander Campbell. This had long been one of the major churches in the Southwest, along with the Methodists and Baptists. The two next-door families went to different Disciples' churches. That favored by the uncle and aunt was located close to the largest Baptist church in the world, where the Reverend George W. Truett, later to figure in an academic freedom controversy involving Henry Smith, preached conservative religious and political doctrines and conducted successful revivals. As an infant, Henry was taken by his mother to choir practice; as a boy, he went every Sunday to church in the morning, then Sunday School, then Christian Endeavor, and again to church at night. In addition there was the Wednesday night prayer meeting. He did not remember any Bible reading at home, but he became reasonably familiar with Scripture through constant exposure in church. The Campbellite church prides itself on its simplicity, and Henry did not hear theological arguments. He thought that his father's religion was based on a simple covenant, scrupulously kept. If you believe the teachings of the church and keep the rules, never lying or cheating or philandering, you will be taken care of in the hereafter. In seasons of revival, religious feeling was aroused through hymns like "Why Not Today," and "Jesus Is Tenderly Calling You Home." When Henry was about twelve, he announced his willingness to go forward and acknowledge his salvation. He did this mainly to please his mother, and when I talked to him he was sure that he never felt religious emotion. He came to find the preachers he heard ungrammatical and illogical, and at fifteen, in his first defiance of his father, he announced that he was going to stop being a regular churchgoer. Somewhat to his surprise, this decision was accepted.

In politics the Smiths were conservative Democrats. Texas politics in those days were a matter of skilled in-fighting among Democratic factions. Woodrow Wilson, not the most congenial Democrat for Texans, was the focus of patriotic support during World War I. When Henry entered High school in 1918, ROTC training was compulsory. His OD uniform was scratchy, and since at twelve he was small for his age, his rifle was nearly as tall as he was. He was drilled "until hell wouldn't hold it," and went to summer ROTC camp at Lampasas. There he heard, from the regular army instructors, the dirtiest language he has ever heard anywhere, complete with homosexual invitations he did not then understand. In respectable circles, of course, sex was absolutely impossible to discuss. Even the preachers went no further than vaguely to urge the importance of purity.

Henry remembered his childhood and early adolescence as an unexciting, mildly depressing period. There was no real suffering or oppression, and indeed his good grades and generally unrebellious behavior brought him the approval of his elders if not of his contemporaries. Yet he remembered these years as monotonous, and guilt-ridden, with few pleasures. Such memories are common among those who grew up as precocious children in small-town America near the turn of the century. In all parts of the country, boys and girls growing up in very simple ways were about to encounter startling ideas, often in public libraries, sometimes in colleges, sometimes in first visits to big cities. As a result they rebelled against their background, often painfully. At a considerable psychic price some of them emerged as poets, novelists, historians, critics, and sociologists.

In these years this was happening especially often in the South. C. Vann Woodward, two years younger than Henry Smith, perhaps the leading American historian of his generation, grew up about 150 miles from Dallas in Vanndale, Arkansas. His liberation began at Atlanta and Chapel Hill, where he read Mencken and other iconoclasts and, a little later, had some contact with the Agrarians and Southern regionalists. The result was a historical stance toward the Southern past that was harshly critical but also intermittently defensive. A few years earlier, W. J. Cash, whose brilliant and ironic *Mind of the South* Woodward disapproves of but Smith admired, had grown up in a mill town in piedmont South Carolina. Cash too read the *American Mercury* and the new literature and repudiated some, but by no means all, of the Southern myth he analyzed so trenchantly. As Henry Smith would have been the first to point out, North Texas was not South Carolina or even Arkansas, yet there is a good deal in common in the life stories of Cash, Woodward, and Smith.

In 1922, at sixteen, Henry Smith started a new phase of his life by entering Southern Methodist University. This institution, like all provincial colleges then, had the great virtue, now generally unappreciated, of being undemanding. In most courses, one read a textbook and the same material was repeated in lectures. Either going to lectures or reading the textbook was quite enough; for a bright boy or girl both would be a waste of time. This left one free to read, talk to people, and grow up.

Henry Smith remembered three really good teachers at SMU. One, in the School of Theology, taught New Testament; a second taught the philosophy of religion. It was necessary at SMU to be cautious with these subjects, but Smith was introduced to the complex issues and profound scholarly arguments arising out of higher criticism and the historical study of the Bible. The other outstanding teacher was John H. McGinnis, probably the person who most deeply influenced the early life and thought of Henry Smith. McGinnis was one of those literary intellectuals who in those days found themselves on college and university faculties even though they were not inclined toward research. A teacher and critic rather than a scholar, McGinnis was eclectic, skeptical, and lively-minded. He was one of the first to recognize the quality of William Faulkner, whose first novels were just coming out. Passionately interested in the landscape, culture, and literature of the region he lived in, McGinnis was to become editor of the *Southwest Review* in 1927, and Henry Smith was to serve as an associate editor for ten years. Already, when Smith was an undergraduate, McGinnis made him his assistant on the book page of the *Dallas Morning News*.

Like other colleges and universities, SMU in this period had a few students of intellectual tastes who banded together in rejection of the dominant collegiate culture of sports and fraternities. To judge from Henry Smith's anecdotes, that culture at SMU, where not only liquor but also dances were forbidden, was quite as coarse and raunchy as at other colleges, with spice added by rule-breaking. In his sophomore year, since his father's business was doing better in the good times of the mid-twenties, Henry went to live in a fraternity house, which had at least the advantage of getting him away from home and its restrictions. One of his memories of fraternity life is of a brother from the Arkansas chapter who was recovering from a severe case of gonorrhea, and was taken care of by the pledges. Feeling no attraction for the fraternity kind of wenching, Henry Smith fell desperately and romantically in love with a girl who was engaged to someone else, but for years gave Henry just enough encouragement to keep him unhappy.

Henry Smith's group of intellectual friends included Lon Tinkle, later professor of French at SMU and semi-official impresario of high culture in Dallas. Another was John Chapman, who introduced Smith to Melville's works and was to become a professor of medicine. A third, Henry's roommate, was James G. Allen, who, though he could not read a note of music, was supporting himself by leading a jazz band. Through him, Henry acquired a lifelong taste for American popular music of various kinds. At the same time he was learning to listen to Beethoven, Chopin, and Schumann, whose works were endlessly played in the practice rooms in the McFarlin Auditorium, where the offices of the *Southwest Review* were located.

Of course this tiny intellectual set read the *American Mercury* and were intrigued to learn that they were living in the Sahara of the Bozart. With glee they applied Mencken's strictures to what they saw around them, but they did not welcome patronizing criticism of Texas by outsiders. I think that in Henry Smith's case the Mencken influence was especially significant. Mencken's detailed knowledge of American popular culture and his love-hate relation with it are reflected in a number of Henry Smith's works. Probably some of this came to Mencken from Mark Twain, whose mixture of affection and revulsion toward a series of squalid river towns was eventually to be discussed in detail by Henry Smith.

The tiny intellectual group at SMU in the twenties tried their hands at writing poetry and read their efforts to each other. Scorning team sports, they played serious tennis. They read and discussed the new American writers: Cather, Cabell ("complete corn" in Henry's later judgment), Lewis, Hemingway, and Faulkner. This was the twenties, not the thirties, and the group's rebellion took the form of aesthetic hostility to bourgeois materialism rather than direct social criticism. There were as far as Henry remembers no Marxists around, yet somehow Henry Smith himself got started on a journey toward the Left. Perhaps this was in opposition to his

father, who, reflecting the increased conservatism of
boom-time Texas and of his big-business customers, was
a fervent supporter of the open shop campaign against
unions. By 1928, three years after graduation, Henry
was to vote for Norman Thomas.

After graduation in 1925 Henry spent a year as a
teaching assistant and *Southwest Review* staff member. He
was getting letters from Allen, who had gone to Harvard
and described Cambridge and Boston ecstatically. The
pull of Harvard must have been increased by the fact
that Uncle Randolph had been there and had sent his
son, Henry's former neighborhood rival. Harvard accepted Henry's application for graduate work in English
only provisionally, and would not give him a scholarship,
since it did not recognize degrees from SMU. With his
father's support, Henry set out in 1926 for Cambridge,
crossing the Mississippi for the first time. From this time
on Harvard was to become one of the two major poles
in Henry's life, competing with the strong pull of Texas,
at first feebly, later much more powerfully.

It is easy to imagine the fascination, for young Smith
from Dallas, of the Boston Symphony, opera, and theater, the Boston Museum of Fine Arts, and especially
Widener Library, vast, beautifully organized, and superbly usable. Of Cambridge gentilities and snobberies,
a student living in a graduate dormitory learned nothing
whatever. Smith's teachers were world-famous scholars,
including George Lyman Kittredge, Irving Babbitt, John
Livingston Lowes, J. S. P. Tatlock, and others hardly less
distinguished. With none of them did Henry Smith ever
exchange a sentence. His most interesting course was
the history of criticism with Babbitt, whose rigorous tra-
ditionalist views Smith respected and rejected. His small-
est course, Kittredge's elementary Anglo-Saxon, had
seventy-five students. Kittredge expected all students to

be in their seats when he entered. He proceeded to call on individual students for translations. If one told him in advance one was unprepared, one was spared his formidable sarcasm, but this could not happen often. As Memorial Hall clock struck the end of the hour, Kittredge walked out the door, speeding to his study.

The Harvard graduate system, then and for some time, was to admit far more first-year students than the University had any expectation of keeping on as doctoral students. The group was weeded by the simple system of piling on a crushing load of work the first year. Henry Smith survived this ordeal by grim concentration and discipline, getting all A's and losing twenty-five pounds. He learned a lot about early English literature. He had, however, been sufficiently inoculated by McGinnis with skepticism and modernity to know that the Harvard approach to literature was old-fashioned. The overwhelming emphasis was on the historical evolution of English from its Germanic and Romance roots, with no hint of the new analytical linguistics already surfacing in Europe.

Smith was offered a second-year scholarship. When he found that in his second year his program would consist of Old French, Old Norse, Middle High German, Gothic, and Middle English, he decided to go back to Texas. An M.A., which was sufficient for teaching at SMU, was already earned and would shortly be formally awarded. Smith left Harvard this time with few regrets. He had, after all, achieved a lot. He knew from this time on that he could work hard enough and had enough ability to make it in the big league. He had a new sense of the heights of prestige and respect to which professors could rise. He went back to Texas, moreover, confident that he had a possible escape route. His performance made it possible for him to go back to Harvard graduate school, should he ever decide to do so.

For the present and for the foreseeable future, Smith in 1927 accepted not unwillingly the prospect of being a teacher, critic, and general man of letters in Dallas. For the next ten years he pursued this program with incredible, almost appalling energy.

Dallas in these years was growing and changing. The population reached 159,000 in 1920, and 260,000 in 1930. The growth of the oil industry in Texas had already begun to change Dallas in the twenties. In 1930 the enormous East Texas oilfield was opened up by Dad Joiner's big strike, and Dallas soon displaced Tulsa as the oil capital of the world. Oil, and the other industries it stimulated, made enormous fortunes for some citizens of Dallas. (According to one local historian, cotton people and cattle people excluded oil people from such prestigious institutions as the Shakespeare Club.) New wealth meant more money for culture—for private art collections, for the theater, for a symphony, for the University, and even a little for the *Southwest Review*. The most lively cultural institution was the little theater, which won national awards and put on Shaw, Ibsen, and O'Neill as well as light comedies. In January 1929 we find Henry Smith writing an essay for the Little Theater program in which he praises the amateur spirit and says, in something a little like the tone of Carol Kennicott, that the deepest purpose of the Little Theater is "to endow life on these prairies with a grace beyond the business of getting a living." Actually Smith had a mixed view of the new Dallas and its cultural possibilities. On the one hand, he threw himself into the effort to bring Dallas into the world of arts and letters; on the other, he was seldom unaware for long of the increase of crass display and the intensifying of reactionary politics that went with the new opulence.

All Smith's literary tasks had to be carried on in time saved from an exhausting round of teaching. During most of this period he taught two sections of freshman English (in which each student wrote a seven-page weekly theme), one sophomore survey of English literature, and one advanced class, sometimes patterned on Babbitt's Harvard class in the history of criticism, though certainly without Babbitt's classicist polemics. Those who have experienced this sort of teaching assignment, carried on without assistants to read papers, know what a numbing burden it can be, particularly for a teacher who takes his work seriously.

Assisting McGinnis on the book page of the *Dallas Morning News* brought fifteen dollars a week and a lot more hard work. It was necessary for Smith to look through the weekly batch of new books, choose some of the heavier reviews for himself, find amateur reviewers for the others and go over their work. Among the books he reviewed were such disparate items as Malcolm Cowley's *Exile's Return* (he liked it, but took the opportunity to point out that university scholars had abandoned modern literature to young essayists), Walter Lippmann's *Preface to Morals* (Lippmann seemed to have gone over to the New Humanists, though he was much deeper than Irving Babbitt), and Paul Buck's *Road to Reunion* (Smith found his treatment of sectional reconciliation much too cheerful and sentimental). The style of the reviews is straightforward and readable, both less academic and less ironical than Smith's later academic work.

By far the chief focus of Smith's literary energies in this period was the *Southwest Review,* of which he was an associate editor or editor throughout the decade 1927–37. In a retrospective article written in 1955, which is perhaps his most exuberant piece of writing, Smith expresses his pride in the *Review* and his affection for McGinnis, its leading spirit. He describes his work on the *Review* as "a chapter—the principal chapter—in my education." McGinnis ran the magazine, Smith told me, as a sort of seminar. Rigorous standards of content, language, and typography often kept him and his young protégés at work in the *Review* office until two or three in the morning. A very small subsidy from the University had to be supplemented by passing the hat for printing and other costs. Reliance on private donors of course necessitated some caution in subject matter; the magazine left religion alone and its occasional political articles dealt with the Al Smith campaign, the early Roosevelt program, or the problems of foreign policy in fairly neutral tones. Though the overwhelming emphasis of the *Review* was regional, there were occasional general literary articles—Sadakichi Hartmann's reminiscences of Whitman, even Irving Babbitt on Dr. Johnson.

Regionalism, as distinct from nineteenth-century local color, was new and exciting in this period, and much in need of definition. In July 1929 the editors asked a number of contributors to answer a somewhat loaded question, "Do you think the Southwestern landscape and common traditions can (or should) develop a culture recognizable as unique, and more satisfying and profound than our present imported culture and art?" The answers received are too many and different to summarize, but Henry Smith had already answered it for himself in an essay on "Culture" published in the Winter 1928 issue. Surveying the current rise of interest in literature and art in Texas, he comes down firmly on the side of culture as a native artifact.

Of course there must always be contact with older civilizations, and with contemporary civilizations in other parts of the world; we can never understand our own environment save against the background afforded by an intimate knowledge of the life and thought of other nations. But this is not the primary thing. . . . There is about the enterprises of the new artistic revival an air of unreality and detachment from the life of Texas. To paraphrase Santayana's criticism of the New England school, these activities lack roots and fresh sap; for their audiences, culture is an intentional acquirement, not the inevitable flowering of a fresh experience. . . . Something must convince the run of those beginning to be attracted to art that Texas culture, paradoxical though the statement seems, cannot become universal until it exhausts the actual, until it sends down its roots where it lives to the center.

Smith was only twenty-two when he wrote this, and would certainly have expressed himself differently later, and yet I think something survived of this early belief in the complementary relation of world tradition and local originality. It should be noticed that Texas culture here and elsewhere is contrasted with *European* culture; Smith's loyalties at this time skipped New York, and his view of Boston was mixed.

Most of the *Review* dealt with the art, literature, folklore, and geography of a region that included Texas, Oklahoma, and New Mexico. Among the frequent contributors were Mary Austin, one of the first writers to deal with "The Land of Little Rain," and J. Frank Dobie, the aficionado of cowboy culture who, Smith said, along with McGinnis, opened his eyes to the significance of the West within American society. The two elements in Southwestern culture treated most frequently were the Indian and the Hispanic. Very little was said about blacks. The cattle kingdom was much discussed, the oil empire not. Two series of articles, one on early naturalists of the Southwest and one on Texas missions, were among the first publications of the Southern Methodist University Press, which Smith helped to found.

To Smith as to his mentor McGinnis, the Southwest emphatically excluded the Old South. In a "Note on the Southwest" published in the Spring 1929 issue of the *Review* he made the difference specific. "I despair," said Smith, "of conveying to an Easterner or even to a Virginian the sense of strangeness with which a Southwesterner visits New Orleans, say, or reads the books coming out of the Deep South of song and story." Though most of the population of the Southwest came from the Southeast, and though Texans were used to seeing cotton fields, the old culture based on slavery could not be transplanted. The landscape, the flora, and the economy of the Southwest were different, and the region's past was Spanish and Indian rather than Confederate. Smith acknowledged that the Southern Renaissance in literature was well ahead of anything happening in the Southwest, but insisted that any Southwestern flowering had to come, however slowly, from Southwestern roots. As an outsider, I find it easy to agree with Smith about the difference between Dallas and New Orleans, not quite as easy to see the similarity between Dallas or Houston or Tulsa on the one hand, and Santa Fe and Taos on the other.

In 1932 the compatibility between South and Southwest was put to an interesting test when the *Southwest Review* was merged with the *Southern Review*, published in Baton Rouge by Louisiana State University. This had the advantage of doubling the subsidy and bringing to the board of editors such distinguished critics as Robert Penn Warren and Cleanth Brooks. The Dallas and Baton Rouge editors met together, often in Shreveport, and despite their differences Warren became a lifelong friend of Henry Smith. In 1934, Smith contributed to the magazine a dry and skeptical analysis of Agrarianism, the essentially nostalgic program put forth by twelve Southern writers, including Warren, in 1930.

For three years the *Review* suffered from a split personality. The same issue could contain an article on Davy Crockett by Constance Rourke and an analysis of T. S. Eliot by Cleanth Brooks. Warren and Brooks ran the review section of the combined *Review*, and in April 1935 McGinnis and presumably Smith were upset by a favorable review of Stark Young's *So Red the Rose*. The reviewer took to task those who are skeptical or contemptuous of the Old South. Southerners had at least been sufficiently realistic "to recognize what lay behind abolitionism, and to fight rather than submit to it." Further sectional hostilities were avoided when, shortly after the Stark Young argument, an amicable divorce was arranged between the Baton Rouge and Dallas elements of the magazine. The *Southern Review* started over with a lavish subsidy from Huey Long's LSU, while the *Southwestern Review* returned to the McGinnis-Smith definition of its region.

One deep-South writer both McGinnis and Smith admired without qualification was William Faulkner, whom both had reviewed favorably long before he was widely admired. In 1932, McGinnis asked Faulkner for a story, and Faulkner sent one called "Miss Zilphia Gant." This is a powerful story of a sexually frustrated and obsessed woman in a small Southern town. When it arrived in Dallas, McGinnis found it too long for the *Review*, and Smith remembered, he also knew that "the bishop wouldn't like it." McGinnis hit on the brilliant expedient of persuading Mr. Stanley Marcus, of Neiman-Marcus, to publish the Faulkner story in one of the elegant and expensive little volumes put out by Marcus's Texas Book Club. Faulkner was paid $250, which he was glad to get.

Smith went to Oxford, Mississippi (by air, with many stops and transfers), to meet Faulkner and complete negotiations. He wrote a seven-page introduction to the Book Club edition of "Miss Zilphia Gant," a story not published again for almost forty years.

Shortly after completing this transaction Smith went with a class of education students and their professor on a summer trip to Oxford—this time Oxford, England. His function, which give him a free trip, was to legitimate the junket by lecturing on Milton and giving examinations. This duty completed, Smith took off with a friend on a walking tour of the Black Forest, winding up in Paris. There he found a letter from his department head telling him that his connection with the University was severed. It was impossible for a Christian institution to tolerate on its faculty a man associated with any writer as foul and lascivious as William Faulkner.

This department head, whom Henry remembered as both an arch-conservative and a natural tyrant, sent letters to all local ministers, denouncing what he saw as part of an attempt to steal SMU from Christ. Henry left for home sooner than he intended and found that he was not without allies. For one thing, Marcus had sponsored the Faulkner publication, and "in Dallas you don't kick Stanley Marcus in the teeth." Eminent lawyers who were fellow members with Smith of a dining club offered him their services free in a suit against the University. The president of SMU, no fool, found that the young professor had some real local clout. He worked out an ingenious compromise. Smith was put on salaried leave for a semester, and after this transferred from the English Department to a newly organized Department of Comparative Literature, where he cheerfully settled down to teaching world classics in translation. Henry Smith's manner in talking about this early battle, his first but not his last involvement in an academic freedom case, was light-hearted and a little triumphant.

In addition to his teaching, his newspaper reviewing, and his editorial duties, Smith in these years imposed on himself a demanding program of reading. Full of the American intellectual's reverence for Europe, and committed to the belief that one cannot understand one's own region or country without some deep exposure to other cultures, he set about teaching himself French and German, slowly working his way through major literary works. He subscribed to critical periodicals in both languages. Before the trip to the Black Forest and Paris, he had managed another European journey. In 1930 he and his friend Lon Tinkle got passage on a freighter for seventy dollars. Tinkle attended classes at the Sorbonne while Smith went to Munich, where he lived for six weeks in a cold *Pension* where nobody spoke English, and went to the opera and concerts.

The principal fields of his most serious reading were anthropology and philosophy, centering, he told me, in the area of epistemology and myth where the two meet. Among the philosophers, perhaps the one who probably influenced Smith the most was the phenomenologist Hans Vaihinger, who dealt with the relation between various types of reality and our perceptions of them. He and others left Smith with a deep suspicion of the primacy of the concrete "fact," a principle still assumed by most academic historians. He also read Henri Bergson, another opponent of nineteenth-century positivism and simple materialism, especially his *Deux Sources de la religion et la morale.* He read carefully the two large volumes of *Das Kapital,* he told me, but was not deeply influenced by Marx. He was especially fascinated by literary and anthropological treatments of the meaning of myth, including Thomas Mann's Joseph series, Sir James Frazer's

Golden Bough, and the writings of Jessie Weston and Lu-
cién Lévy-Bruhl. Arthur Lovejoy's *Great Chain of Being*
furnished a compelling example of the enterprise of
tracing a single idea through many successive minds. (An
academic generation later this enterprise was much
questioned, in Lovejoy's case and also in Smith's.)

Somehow Smith found time for regular tennis and
even for courtship and marriage. He met Elinor Lucas
first as a student in one of his freshman sections and a
bit later in a bookstore. They were married in April
1936.

By this time Smith was getting ready to leave Dallas
again. The effort to foster a regional culture did not
seem as promising as it had. The domination of Texas
by big money was ever more obvious. In 1937 he heard
that Harvard was offering a new degree in American
Civilization without the pedantic linguistic requirements
of the English degree a decade earlier. The new program
was actually set up by president James Bryant Conant
against the will of the English Department and in connection with the Harvard Tercentenary. Conant called
Howard Mumford Jones from Michigan to Harvard as
a professor of American literature, and Jones, who was
a member of the *Southwest Review* editorial board and
had been interviewed by Smith for the *Dallas Morning
News,* was able to get Smith a part-time job teaching
freshman English at Harvard. He arrived back in Cambridge in 1937, a beginning graduate student in American Civilization, a field in which both his academic
knowledge and his practical experience were already
considerable.

Well beyond the limits of the new doctoral program,
the study of American culture at Harvard was in a period
of flowering. At the center were such splendidly creative
literary scholars and teachers as Perry Miller, F. O. Mat-

thiessen, and Kenneth Murdock. Smith found these men free of the old-fashioned genteel assumptions about literature that he had encountered among many of the professors at SMU. The group of graduate students, tutors, and junior faculty that surrounded these professors was equally brilliant—polished, cultivated, supremely articulate, and politically radical. They too were different from their counterparts in Texas, some of them at once more upper class in origin and more deeply alienated from American society than anybody Smith had known. This was just before the end of the Popular Front period of the thirties and some of Smith's closest associates were, we now know, members of the Communist party. Some others agreed closely with the Communists on many issues. Smith found this group immensely stimulating but felt no impetus to join the Party. For one thing, its rigid kind of Marxism seemed to him bound by the same naïve assumptions about "fact" and culture that were taken for granted by standard nonradical historians under the influence of Turner's frontier theory—assumptions he had rejected. Moreover, he was too busy to take a leading part in political argument. Unlike most graduate students then, he was married, and in March 1939 a son was born. The graduate student rumor was that Mayne Smith was born during the exact hours that Henry Smith was taking (and passing) his doctor's orals. If this is not literally true, it may serve as an example of a myth with some symbolic validity. Smith was, as always, working hard in a highly organized manner, pushing ahead with his studies while managing to support his family with a series of junior teaching jobs, fellowships, and loans from his mother (his father died in 1938).

I was a graduate student in History then, and knew, somewhat from the outside, the American Civilization and American Literature group. I remember Henry as a little different from the others. He was not aloof, and not obviously tied to the graduate-student treadmill, and he was always more than willing to throw himself into a discussion of books, politics, or ideas. Yet he seemed to some of us not only a bit older but also better organized, more confident, cooler and more ironical. His Texas accent and Southern politeness also distinguished him from most of his peers.

The professor that influenced Smith most was not one of the sophisticated stars of the English Department but the historian Frederick Merk, who taught a famous, infinitely well-informed, and factually oriented course and seminar on the Westward movement. As Smith put it,

> I realize that it was precisely the impact of Merk's vigorously factual approach to Western history on my earlier flights into the stratosphere of epistemology that set in motion the mental process that became *Virgin Land.*

His dissertation, the first in the new field, took shape out of Smith's courses and his earlier interests. In his first year, in a seminar taught by Howard Mumford Jones, Smith—like the other students—had the task of analyzing a single work of James Fenimore Cooper, in his case one of Cooper's less-known works, *Wyandotte, or, the Hutted Knoll: A Tale.* In Widener, to his great satisfaction, it was possible, as in very few places in this pre-microprint period, to read the original reviews, mostly in New England magazines. This set Smith thinking about Eastern attitudes toward Western material. The next year in a seminar with Merk he chose the topic of the entry into literature of the cowboy, and again pursued this topic mainly in New England magazines, this time magazines of the late nineteenth century. In discussions with Merk and Jones, who together became his doctoral committee, he took on the topic of Eastern perceptions of the West, and started the impossible task of reading all the sources for this vast topic—books, magazines, newspapers, promotional pamphlets, emigrants' guides, and government reports. In 1940, when his money and therefore his time at Harvard was running out, his committee was humane enough to let him cut the thesis off at 1850 and lay down his pencil, "almost as if the noon whistle had blown." He was to continue to work on this project off and on for another decade, often in touch with his teachers. A few years later, for instance, he sent Merk a long piece, very carefully written and researched, on the influence on public policy of the optimistic and mistaken belief that the climate of the dry plains was changing for the better, an example in his view of the "traditional American contempt for experts and theorists" and of the malign influence of beliefs that conflict with demonstrable fact.

In 1940, Henry, Elinor, and Mayne left for the long drive back to Dallas. Unmarried and nine years younger, I was enormously impressed when he told me that at meal stops it was his practice to walk through a restaurant to the men's room, carrying Mayne under one arm and a potty-chair in the other hand. This seemed to me an example of unbelievable heroism.

Smith remained on the SMU faculty and the *Southwest Review* for only one year. He received and accepted an invitation to move to the University of Texas, at Austin, as Professor of English and American History. Austin had many attractions. Friends who had written for the *Southwest Review* were among them—one was J. Frank Dobie, another Walter Prescott Webb, whose compelling and romantic history of the great plains bears directly on some of the issues treated in *Virgin Land*. The uni-

versity had received widespread gifts of land from
Texas, which unlike other states owned its own empty
lands. On one piece owned by the university, oil had
been found, and there was money enough to finance
many buildings and even a relatively good library. Af-
fluence did not, however, extend to faculty salaries or
teaching loads; the legislature was niggardly in these
matters and Smith taught as many courses at Austin as
he had at Dallas. The town was much smaller, the landscape far less bleak. On the whole, Smith thought he
might remain in Austin the rest of his life.

Shortly before he got there, however, a desperate
struggle had begun between the liberal president, Homer P. Rainey, and the ultraconservative regents appointed by Governor Wilbert Lee (Pappy) O'Daniel, who
had campaigned with a hillbilly band and an anti-New
Deal program. The issues of this conflict were such that
it was impossible for Smith to remain aloof, and the
balance of forces such that no quick victory like his own
at Dallas in 1932 was possible.

In one of many incidents, three young economists
were dismissed by regential intervention because they
had tried to read the text of the Fair Labor Standards
Act at a patriotic meeting against that statute. It was
wartime and the Reverend George W. Truett of Dallas,
who sat on the platform, accused the young economists
of having, by this action, insulted the Gold Star mothers,
some of whom were present at the meeting. Another
tempest boiled up over an issue closer to Smith's concerns. *The Big Money,* the third volume of Dos Passos's
U.S.A., had been put on the reading list for a course in
writing for engineering students, and the regents found
the book obscene and subversive. President Rainey, a
fighter by temperament, struck back with a public denunciation of the regents for violating freedom of

thought and expression and interfering in administrative details contrary to good procedure. The regents summarily dismissed the president, who was strongly supported by the students and most of the liberal arts faculty.

I was at this time in the Navy in the Pacific. In a letter of April 19, 1945, Henry wrote me that the regents were surprised at the "unshirted hell" raised by their action and that for the moment the affair was at a stand-off. He knew he might have to leave Austin but hoped this would not happen; in many ways he liked the place. He was one of the executive committee of eleven supporting the president, up to his neck in meetings and pamphlets. Obviously not much progress was being made on the book that was growing out of his thesis. Smith was rescued from this situation for two years, first by an invitation to teach at Harvard the course and seminar usually taught by Perry Miller, on leave in Europe; then by a fellowship at the Huntington Library.

At the Huntington Library in 1946–47, *Virgin Land* finally took shape. The Huntington had a wonderful collection of Western dime novels, and Smith's attention had been called to this genre by an article of Merle Curti, suggesting their importance for understanding American popular culture. He set to work reading them one after the other. When he told me this I commiserated with him for having to plow through this depressing material, but I was wrong. Smith, in what seems to me a Menckenian manner, always found the careful study of subliterature fascinating. Indeed, he was not to deal with a writer he really admired until his later work on Mark Twain. The Huntington was also the repository for the papers of Frederick Jackson Turner, and Smith realized that the theorist of the frontier had to be the subject of his last chapter.

During this two-year absence the battle at Austin had been fought and lost. In 1946 former president Rainey campaigned for the Democratic nomination for the governorship and was overwhelmingly defeated by a conservative candidate. All the issues of the university fight played a part in the campaign, and Henry once told me that some people in Texas believed that *The Big Money* was a dirty book actually *written* by Rainey. A compliant nonentity was appointed president and some faculty members started to leave.

In 1947, Henry Smith was invited to become Professor of English at the University of Minnesota and he decided, with considerable inner conflict, to say goodbye to Texas. He wrote a letter to the *Daily Texan* explaining the reasons for his departure. He clearly hated to run out on a fight, and predicted, wrongly, that the faculty would eventually win their battle. His reason for leaving was that he could get no work done in a situation where every week brought a new insult to the faculty, a new challenge that had to be met.

In Minnesota, where he was to remain until he came to Berkeley in 1953, Smith set about trying to get a publisher for *Virgin Land*. He sent it first to Bernard De Voto at Houghton Mifflin, then to Alfred Knopf. Both firms had much that was flattering to say about the book, but believed that it had no possibilities for trade-book sales (strictly speaking, they were right, though the book was eventually to sell well over 100,000 copies, mostly for use in history courses). Finally, after long consideration, the book was accepted by Harvard in the Fall of 1949 and published in 1950. One result of the fact that it had been read by various scholars for three presses was that even before publication a lot of people knew that something important was on the way. It was my strong impression at the time that everybody I met who was concerned with American studies knew about *Virgin Land* and its author, even though he had published very little outside his region. The overwhelmingly favorable reception of the book when it finally appeared needs no discussion here, nor does its powerful effect on a generation of scholars in its field.

With all the praise, *Virgin Land* has also received a certain amount of criticism, much of it centering on such problems as the relation of myth to "reality," the alleged reification of an idea or image transferred through many minds over a long period, the difficulty of ascribing beliefs or motives to "most people," or "the popular mind." These are the criticisms brought against many kinds of literary and intellectual history in recent years. Like most authors who have worked hard on a book and then find its very basis under attack, Smith sometimes defended himself. He pointed out, correctly, that he had thought and read about just this kind of epistemological issue for years before he had started work on *Virgin Land*. His most effective defense, I think, is his frank admission that some of these problems cannot be impeccably solved; to demand that they must be is to call for an end to all history of culture.

I do not want to take part in this argument here. My purpose in writing this paper has been to suggest that the book owes its continuing vitality (and perhaps some of its vulnerability also) to the life history of its writer. Above all, *Virgin Land* reflects the deep and fertile ambivalence of Henry Nash Smith's attitude toward the East and the West, Harvard and Dallas, European tradition and Western regionalism, and especially toward American popular culture, which fascinated and repelled him much as it did H. L. Mencken and Mark Twain. It was the book his life had prepared him to write.

3

The Prophet and the Establishment

Reviewing Richard Fox's biography of Reinhold Niebuhr* gave me an opportunity to reread the Niebuhr books that had influenced me most, and to rethink the nature of his influence on me and on many historians of my generation. The review is reprinted by permission of Reviews in American History.

To the post-World War II intellectual generation, Reinhold Niebuhr was a towering figure. A few condemned him for pessimism and obscurantism. Many more, inside and outside the churches, found his message of contrition and limitation sustaining and helpful. In the fifties he was the favorite theologian of a large number of political intellectuals, some of them in positions of power. Some of these tried, never with complete success, to separate his social and political teachings from their Biblical and theological foundations. In the next period, associated by revisionist historians with the cold war,

*Richard Wightman Fox. *Reinhold Niebuhr: A Biography.* New York: Pantheon, 1985. x + 325 pp. Photographs, notes, bibliography, and index. $19.95.

Niebuhr lost much of his following. Since his death in 1971 he has had both admirers and detractors.

Partly because of the passage of time and the cooling of some political arguments of the postwar period, and partly also because of the author's massive and scrupulous research in Niebuhr's scattered papers, this biography by Richard W. Fox is the most objective to date. Fox brings out, sometimes in painful detail, Niebuhr's shortcomings. This is much to the author's credit. Even more admirable is the fact that Fox's objective examination does not in the end leave Reinhold Niebuhr diminished.

Few of Niebuhr's admirers would deny that the enormous mass of his published work, twenty books and hundreds of uncollected articles, is uneven. He was often imprecise in language, careless with definitions, high-handed with sources. Even his devoted brother Richard, a more modest and careful and—some think—a more profound theologian, when he was asked why Reinhold published so much more than he did, once snapped, "I think before I write" (p. 237; the whole subject of the relation between the brothers is one of this book's best developed themes). Fox makes even clearer than Niebuhr's other biographers the immediate cause of so much hasty work: Niebuhr's compulsive and driven way of life. From his emergence in the late twenties as a national figure, through his decades of gathering fame, all the way to his predictable crippling stroke in 1952, Niebuhr's schedule of college sermons, lectures, board meetings, and political involvements makes it hard to believe that he had time to write any books at all. Heroic and self-destructive, Niebuhr put his students first; his preaching, lecturing, and political activities second. After these came his writing, then his family and friends—loved but sometimes neglected—and last of all, himself.

This perpetual activism and its cost in depth is not

the only blemish brought out in Fox's careful and generally convincing portrait. Niebuhr, as Fox describes him, cared more about power, success, and popularity than his theology of contrition allowed for. He could reply harshly to criticism, though he usually calmed down and regretted such episodes. Despite his commitment to democracy, he often let slip an elitist phrase, indicating that what was most important was beyond the understanding of most people. Somewhat rigid about sex, he was also generally lacking in sensuous appreciation of art or life. His colleague Paul Tillich once complained that Niebuhr wouldn't even take time to look at the spring flowers blooming on the Union Seminary campus. "They were there last year too," answered Niebuhr, rushing to an appointment (p. 257)).

Niebuhr's education was surprisingly meager. His three years at the provincial seminary of a minor denomination were followed by two at the Yale Divinity School, then a less than first-rate institution. His spotty knowledge of history and philosophy and his lack of time for study account for his sometimes mechanical summaries of vast subjects, drawn from textbooks which he was honest enough to cite. Yet there were some advantages to be drawn from the fact that he came relatively late to the major figures that influenced him most: William James, Karl Marx, Augustine, and (usually as an opponent) Karl Barth. His reactions to these powerful stimuli were adult and individual; one by one they were fitted into the moral and intellectual world that had been first formed by the Bible and his early preaching experience. Niebuhr himself, the book makes clear, was acutely conscious of the lacks and faults listed by his biographer. His self-knowledge, sometimes expressed in moving terms, saved him from arrogance.

Fox's freshest insights deal with Niebuhr's character

and personal life, but he gives most of his space to the changing political commitments of this busy activist. His treatment of forty years of intellectual politics is well-informed and historically imaginative; he avoids simple judgments of past loyalties. In the pre–1917 beginning, Niebuhr opted strongly for the Americanist side in the divided German-American community. He was never entirely to abandon the second-generation immigrant patriotism expressed by this choice. His support of the First World War and the Wilson administration was ardent and somewhat intolerant. Versailles and a subsequent trip to Germany left him increasingly disillusioned with the "grey compromises" of Wilsonian liberalism, still more with war itself. Like the liberal church leaders he was beginning to know, he moved rapidly in the direction of pacifism.

Fox deals more fully than any other biographer with Niebuhr's formative years as a pastor in Henry Ford's Detroit, usefully supplementing Niebuhr's own appealing and vivid account in his *Leaves from the Notebook of a Tamed Cynic* (1929). Writing steadily for the *Christian Century,* increasingly concerned with city affairs, Niebuhr became involved for the first time in the cause of black Americans. Boldly, he attacked the highly advertised but, as he saw it, phony philanthropy of the Ford organization. Deploring Babbittry, he yet worked harder and more successfully than we had realized to make his church both bigger and better.

Already a prolific and highly visible social critic, Niebuhr was called to Union Seminary in 1928 as Professor of Social Ethics. It was in New York a few years later that he reached the peak of his radicalism, becoming active in the militant wing of the Socialist party. In the early thirties, with the depression at its worst and fascism triumphing in Germany, many intellectuals turned sharply to the left. The Communist party, in this period before the development of the Popular Front, was not the only group condemning compromises with liberalism. Niebuhr was increasingly fed up with the facile pacifism and progressivism of the late Social Gospel, still dominant in the leadership of the mainline liberal churches. In the introduction to his most powerful political polemic, *Moral Man and Immoral Society* (1932), he calls for the first time for "a more radical political orientation and more conservative religious convictions." It is impossible to transfer an ethic of sacrifice from the individual to the social sphere: the necessary social changes will never be achieved by ethical or rational appeal, and it is the working class that understands this best. As for the use of force, there is no valid moral distinction between revolutionary action and the covert coercion practiced by the middle class and its government. In *Reflections on the End of an Era* (1934) Niebuhr's catastrophism reaches a climax. The sickness of Western society is organic and terminal. The rise of fascism, amounting to a last violent defense of capitalism, must come about in America as well as Europe. The New Deal is dismissed, as is Keynes, whom Niebuhr lumps together with Stuart Chase and other deluded social scientists. (This is the only major book he decided later not to reprint.)

Yet even in this period, as Fox makes clear, Niebuhr never completely admired the Soviet Union and never accepted the Leninist millennium of the classless society. The poor must come to power, but they are likely to fall into the error of vindictiveness. Fanatics are necessary in this crisis but must somehow, in some complicated manner, eventually be brought under the rule of reason.

As war came closer, Niebuhr gradually backed away from catastrophism and, more slowly, from socialism.

What mattered now was the defeat of fascism. Coalition politics became necessary, the New Deal increasingly acceptable, American pragmatic democracy increasingly admirable. Niebuhr broke with the Socialist party over rearmament. He had already broken, finally and in some cases harshly, with many of his old friends among the liberal church leaders. These men, remembering contritely how the churches had joined the Wilsonian crusade in 1917, could not accept military preparation even against Hitler.

The movement toward the middle was signaled by *The Children of Light and the Children of Darkness* (1944), perhaps the most interesting of Niebuhr's political books. Niebuhr took his text from Luke, "The children of this world are wiser in their generation than the children of light." He takes "the children of light" to mean the idealistic liberals and pacifists; "the children of this world" or of darkness are Machiavellian political realists. A proper balance, retaining some of the virtues of both, can be achieved only by a religious perspective, which will allow us to abandon Utopian delusions while keeping alive, even in this world, ultimate hope. Niebuhr comes down clearly on the side of practical adjustment in politics against Utopianism. Yet the balance is very subtle; he does not surrender as clearly as Fox implies to the children of darkness. The realists have their own delusions, and one of them is to underrate the possibilities for change in a revolutionary situation. Whether, in the rest of his political career, Niebuhr was able to maintain the delicate balance he achieves in this book is a question much debated by recent writers.

It was in the years right after World War II that Niebuhr reached the peak of his influence, not only in religious and academic circles but among some highly placed children of this world. This was a time when

American political intellectuals found themselves in a position of unwonted and unwanted power. The United States was supreme in the world in military might, economic strength, and, many thought, cultural creativity. Many American intellectuals, having recently turned in an anti-Communist direction, found themselves in the uncomfortable position of supporting their own government's foreign policy. Yet even some of the most patriotic of them found themselves under attack by McCarthyites for past radicalism or present liberalism. In this difficult and confusing position, in this period of unprecedented victory and danger, it is not surprising that many American intellectuals found merit in Niebuhr's basic teaching, that it was impossible to avoid assuming world responsibilities, but that those who assume them must be contritely conscious of human limitations.

Naturally enough, Niebuhr's teachings were especially helpful to a number of intellectuals who found themselves in unaccustomed positions of influence, and to some political figures of intellectual tendencies. In the first group were Arthur Schlesinger, Jr. (Niebuhr's close friend), Hans Morgenthau, George Kennan, Walter Lippmann, Will Herberg, and James Reston; in the second Paul Nitze, McGeorge Bundy, Dean Acheson, and, a little later, Hubert Humphrey. He was the favorite theologian, that is, of the Brightest and Best, that group of able and devoted public servants who looked impressive then, were sharply criticized later during the Vietnam War, and perhaps seem somewhat better now in contrast to some of their current successors in power. Niebuhr was taken up also by the Luce magazines, and appeared on the cover of *Time*'s twenty-fifth anniversary issue in 1948.

The Irony of American History, published in 1952, influenced statesmen, publicists, and particularly historians, some of whom were looking around for an alternative to the easy progressivism that still ruled most writing of American history. Both great powers, Niebuhr argues in this book, are caught in a situation of irony, which exists where the best qualities of men and nations lead them into evil. Because both nations imagine themselves entirely just, they are certain to be led into arrogance. Russia, however, because it believes more firmly in the complete goodness of its own program, is led into greater extremes of cruelty. In America, given to constant self-criticism, there is more chance to avoid these extremes. In this situation, it would be a terrible mistake either to withdraw into isolationism or (as some very powerful figures were urging) to use the nuclear threat to compel Russian surrender. Instead of either alternative, America must humbly wait out the course of history, try to understand the sources of resentment and hatred, and perform those actions immediately necessary. The prescription sounds not unlike Kennan's early description of containment.

Niebuhr in the fifties became a regular official consultant for the State Department. He backed the current American position on most issues, including aid to Greece and Turkey, resistance to the Berlin blockade, and NATO. Originally equivocal about the atomic weapon, he approved the making of the hydrogen bomb. He strongly opposed the Wallace campaign in 1984. Always interested in Europe rather than Asia, he thought that the United States should let Taiwan go in order to avoid war in Asia.

How this record is to be evaluated depends on one's position on the issues of those days. Fox takes a sensible middle position on the question whether and to what extent Niebuhr was taken into camp by the liberal policy makers. If I understand this biographer's position correctly (I may be misled because this judgment seems close to my own) Niebuhr's central message, his anti-Utopianism, his rejection both of withdrawal and aggression, seem both intrinsically appealing and relevant to the times. In immediate application, however, these doctrines were sometimes misapplied by his admirers. Moreover, it is hard to deny that he occasionally lost sight of his own basic insights. At times he seems to have verged on the complacency against which he had issued his most powerful warnings. Like many others, he sometimes exaggerated the monolithic solidity of world communism, instead of recognizing that it too was riddled with inconsistency, as well as the degree to which the United States was successfully solving its domestic problems.

In February 1952, worn out by his incessant round of meetings, lectures, and deadlines. Niebuhr suffered a severe stroke. Fox deals compassionately with the remaining nineteen years of his life. He made a valiant effort to resume his teaching, lecturing, and writing, but his work shows the effect of illness and fatigue. And from time to time he went even further in support of cold war policies. He criticized Eisenhower for unwise pacifism, and justified the execution of the Rosenbergs (a position he was to regret later). Despite his friendship with Schlesinger, he was suspicious of the Kennedys on moral grounds. In the last years, during the Nixon presidency, he returned to a position of opposition and, after some hesitation, became a militant critic of the Vietnam War. In the past his patriotic record had not saved him from repeated investigation by Hoover's FBI and periodical attack by anti-Communist extremists. He now became a target of criticism by important intellectuals of the left like Christopher Lasch and major revisionist historians like Walter LaFeber.

Reading Fox's close account of this political odyssey,

it is impossible to see Niebuhr as a profound political leader, kept right on track by his religious insights. He avoided the extreme gyrations of some political intellectuals, and was right and wrong in his particular judgments in about the same proportion as the best of his secular liberal friends. Nor was he a major systematic theologian. He knew this, and indeed often denied that he was a theologian at all. In what, then, lies the greatness that Fox and many others concede to him?

Fox's own answer is I think the right one: Niebuhr was a great preacher. A preacher by definition speaks from a text, and Niebuhr was always at his best when he stuck closest to his Biblical starting point. Again by definition, a preacher speaks to the heart as well as the head. Yet Niebuhr was by no means a revivalist, nor did he admire such contemporaries as Billy Graham. At no time did he seem, even to his devoted followers, filled with the Holy Spirit in the manner of a Wesley or an Edwards. His religion was mostly cerebral; he had no mass following. On the other hand he was not interested in the metaphysics of his colleague Paul Tillich, and found the neo-orthodoxy of Karl Barth far too otherworldly. In theology he was always a liberal, rejecting those he called bone-headed literalists even more sharply than the easy rationalists. The Incarnation was profoundly true as a metaphor for the involvement of the infinite in the temporal; the Resurrection was a great symbol of hope arrived at through suffering.

Niebuhr's central message deals with human nature. It was seldom stated in terms too complicated for his special national congregation, intellectual but not theologically adept. Human beings are finite and limited, but occasionally capable of transcendence. One can be successful only in accepting the inevitability of partial failure. One must do one's best with no hope of ultimate success on earth. To this Sisyphean struggle, nothing is irrelevant. Thus a dualistic separation of religion from daily life is no less an error than a dogmatic materialism. Niebuhr must be judged by the depth and usefulness of this central teaching. He would have been the last to say that it could possibly be correctly applied at all times by anybody. Unlike many prophets of humility he had the grace to extend his consciousness of human error to himself. Fox quotes Niebuhr's own summary of his work in a late letter. "I spoke and wrote all over the place," he says, out of a "tremendous urge to express myself." Much of the result had turned out "slightly cockeyed or partly askew" (p. 295).

Fox, who seems in the course of his work to have picked up some of Niebuhr's taste for paradox, apparently agrees in part with this self-judgment. Yet he also gives Niebuhr credit for a major intellectual achievement, welding together "the tragic sense of life and the quest for justice" (p. 297). He believes that Niebuhr was the last great intellectual preacher, preaching on a circuit that no longer exists. If that is so, we are the poorer. Fox is obviously correct in saying that Niebuhr's social and political teachings cannot be "ripped out of their context and pressed into service today" (pp. 297–98). And yet his basic message seems more badly needed than ever in this period of dangerous national self-righteousness.

Fox has given us a fine biography, superbly researched, well written, and always interesting. It is not a definitive work replacing all others. The other excellent biography, written in 1975 by Paul Merkley, analyzes Niebuhr's major books more closely. June Bingham's 1961 study has both the advantages and disadvantages of a tribute by a warm friend. For the theology, students will turn first to some of the essays collected by

Charles W. Kegley and Robert W. Bretall in 1956. Nothing will ever replace completely Niebuhr's own brief "Intellectual Autobiography" in that volume, a small masterpiece of self-knowledge. As Fox says in his introduction, "it is a sign of his stature that each generation will have to confront him anew."

II Edwards and After

4

Harriet Beecher Stowe's *Oldtown Folks:* An Introduction.

I was delighted when in 1964, I was asked by the John Harvard Library to edit a new edition of Oldtown Folks, *and I enjoyed my work on it more than any piece of writing and research I have done. For one thing, I had long been interested in post-Edwardsian Calvinism and its theological, psychological, and cultural effects. These form the main subject of the novel. For another, I realized in the course of this work that I enjoy making general points through research on particular subjects more than I do writing general essays. And also I wrote the final version of this piece in oddly delightful circumstances, sitting by a peat fire in a cottage in Western Ireland, while the rain poured down outside.*

There are two other even more important reasons. One is that in my research on this book, I experienced the thrill of making a genuine if minor discovery. I had been reading the works of the late Edwardsian, ultra-Calvinist theological theologian, Nathaniel Emmons. I learned that Emmons had played a particularly poignant role in the history of the Beecher family. It occurred to me that "Dr. Stern", in the novel might well be Emmons. A sermon of Dr. Stern's, quoted at length in the novel, seemed familiar in style, and I asked my especially able research assistant, David Lundberg, to look for it in Emmons's collected works. He found it, which took the identification clear out of the realm of conjecture.

The other reason this essay was important to me I learned only later. This was that Emmons had played in the life of my own direct ancestors the same role he had played in the life of the Beechers.* Emmons himself and some of his ultra-Calvinist colleagues had preached his special kind of grimly uncompromising, strangely comforting funeral sermons over a number of my direct ancestors, Mays who lived in Attleborough, Massachusetts, a place where Emmons's kind of Calvinism held out into the nineteenth century. My father was only two generations removed from the strict adherents of this theology, and there is no question that its cultural and theological residue marked his personality. His influence on me had its parallels to Lyman Beecher's influence on his daughter Harriet. It was no coincidence that I had responded emotionally to Stowe's novel about "her own people". A little way back, they were my own people too.

This introduction to the John Harvard edition of the novel (Cambridge, 1966) is reprinted by permission of the Harvard University Press.

In 1865 Harriet Beecher Stowe wrote her friend and publisher, James T. Fields, that she could not accept an invitation from his wife, her dear Annie, to pay a visit. Her reason was that she felt it was finally time to get seriously to work, in quiet and concentration, on the New England novel she had been brooding over for many years.[1] From then on until the book was finished early in 1869 Mrs. Stowe gave herself, her publisher, and her

---

*This is discussed at length in the third chapter of my *Coming to Terms*.

family a very hard time. Her letters to both the Fields are full of apologies, complaints about distractions, hesitations about the title, and exultation about the quality of what was being painfully achieved. In December 1867 she thought that the book was almost done, but in 1868 she was still struggling: "*My own book,* instead of cooling, boils and bubbles daily and nightly, and I am pushing and spurring like fury to get to it. I work like a dray-horse, and I'll *never* get in such a scrape again."[2] On Christmas Eve 1868 she again saw the end in sight, this time correctly, and again insisted she had never put so much work upon anything before. In February 1869 she finally finished the job, still complaining: "I have struggled with every kind of difficulty in writing it, and it has seemed some times as if it were going to take my life to do it, and I wish to live to write two or three more, and intend to, P.P. [Providence permitting?]"[3]

In many authors, all this display of agony and temperament would be part of a standard drama of parturition. Mrs. Stowe, however, had come a long way since she had scribbled *Uncle Tom's Cabin* on her kitchen table in Brunswick under—she later insisted—immediate Divine dictation. She was a well-to-do, prolific, experienced author who could command comfort and solitude either in her new big house in Hartford or her orange grove in far-off, undiscovered Florida. Moreover she was never a meticulous writer; she left it to lesser folk to fuss and fret over style. Why then had she suffered so acutely over *Oldtown Folks?* Partly because she intended, as she repeatedly told the Fields and others, that it should be her masterpiece. Partly, also because of its subject matter. The center of *Oldtown Folks* is the center of Mrs. Stowe's whole life, her long and agonizing struggle with the religion of her fathers, and more particularly with the religion of her father.

She herself did not doubt that the book was worth the struggle; others have made varying judgments. Two important contemporary reviewers were tired of New England. E. L. Godkin's *The Nation,* the new organ of the intellectual and political elite, found the book one more indication of the region's decay. Surely, said the anonymous reviewer in a tone of weary tolerance, we have had enough of the Puritan parson and the deacon "and the Puritan tithing man; and the Puritan Thanksgiving, and 'Lection cake, and May Training; and the Puritan 'revivals,' and 'doctrines,' and 'donation parties' " and the rest of the overworked provincial paraphernalia. Moreover, Mrs. Stowe's characters (especially, the reviewer added, the male characters) were as tired as her plot devices—the mysterious child of vaguely aristocratic antecedents, the brilliant and wicked fascinator, duly punished in the end.[4] Bret Harte, who could not take his dislike of New England as lightly as a New York reviewer, looked forward in an anonymous review in *The Overland Monthly* to the day when "we shall probably hear less of Jonathan Edwards and Governor Winthrop, and even begin to understand that they have as little to do with the present civilization as the aborigines."[5]

Mrs. Stowe was wounded by the *Nation*'s review, but the book was praised by her friend Lowell and her correspondent George Eliot, and there was never any doubt about its popular success. Soon the town of Natick, original of Oldtown, was making money out of visits to places celebrated in the novel, and Mrs. Stowe was at work satisfying the demand for more New England stories, this time narrated by Sam Lawson, the celebrated town loafer of *Oldtown.*[6] Moreover, the book was being imitated; despite the *Nation*'s weariness with New England, literary historians place the book near the beginning of the local color movement rather than at its end. For several generations the book's reputation rose and fell—and mostly it was a slow decline—with the literary fortunes of New England local color in general. Artistically inferior to the work of Sarah Orne Jewett, it was remembered if at all as an early specimen of the genre, and the best of the *other* books by the author of *Uncle Tom's Cabin.*

In the 1920's and 1930's a major re-examination of the American past took place. Its main focus was on literature, and one of its main themes was a bitterly hostile indictment of Puritanism. For the few who read it, *Oldtown Folks* became an important anti-Puritan novel. Constance Rourke's amusing, sometimes penetrating, and sketchy portrait of the Beechers probably did more than any other book to set this pattern.[7] It was powerfully revived in 1962 by Edmund Wilson, who rediscovered Mrs. Stowe along with the American Civil War, and correctly said that Puritanism had a lot to do with both.[8]

Well before this, however, Puritanism was itself being reassessed. Instead of a mere mask for sexual repression or hatred of the arts it began to be seen as a profound effort to come to grips with permanent metaphysical and moral problems, and as the source of much of America's greatest literature. Perry Miller, who played a heroic role in this reassessment, gave it as his opinion that "Harriet Beecher Stowe, brought up in the Edwardsian tradition, understood many of its implications better than the theologians who endeavored to follow him [Edwards], and could evaluate his achievements in terms that are fundamental for understanding American culture."[9] Following his lead, Charles H. Foster in 1954 published a brilliant and thorough survey of the whole body of Mrs. Stowe's writing, concentrating on her deeply ambivalent relation to her ancestral faith and calling *Oldtown Folks* a "central New England and American book."[10] This has become a widespread judgment; yet the book has not been reprinted* and its rediscovery has been largely limited, like that of many American classics, to professional students of the American past.

This continuing neglect does not seem to me surprising. Though I agree with much of the recent praise, especially that of such deeply informed scholars as Miller and Foster, I cannot altogether disagree with the 1869 judgment of the *Nation*. *Oldtown Folks* is not a good novel. It is, however, an important and highly interesting book, in some ways all the more interesting because of its author's limited capacity for invention. Mrs. Stowe lacked creative talent but had in large measure other literary gifts. In the first place she was, as James Russell Lowell told her, one of "the few persons lucky enough to be born with eyes in your head."[11] She was a keen observer and often a penetrating historian. Even more important, she was a Beecher, and therefore first and foremost a preacher. Her treatment of New England Calvinism in *Oldtown Folks* is far more than expert local color; it is more even than intellectual history. It is a record of the intense and painful effort of a gifted woman to find her way through the difficult issues of her day. This effort was carried on in terms of her inherited Calvinist tradition, and illuminates that tradition in a way that no later scholar, looking at Puritanism from outside, could entirely emulate.

Mrs. Stowe, in dealing with declining Calvinism of the early nineteenth century, is not studying a bygone social and religious pattern primarily for literary or scholarly purposes. She is discussing the way a people—and she herself above all—had tried to deal with the perennial problems of the meaning of life and death. By the time

*It has now, as part of the Stowe volume of the Library of America (New York 1983).

she wrote *Oldtown Folks* she had fought her way out—
or almost out—of the thorny tangle of post-Edwardsian
theology. She treats New England religion with respect
and affection, but always wryly. She is not sorry that the
formulations taught in her youth are dead, or almost
dead, but she cannot dismiss the outlook of which these
formulations were a passing symbol. Ambivalence—usually the most fruitful perspective for a historian—had
grown in this instance out of Harriet Beecher's upbringing and Mrs. Stowe's whole experience of life. *Oldtown
Folks* could have been written only when New England
Calvinism was still warm in its grave and its ghost still
walked through the memories and emotions of a generation. To understand the book, to discuss its relation
to historical reality, and to assess its author's achievement
we must look first at the religion in which Mrs. Stowe
was brought up, and then at her own struggle with its
stern teachings.

For Harriet Beecher, as for most of her generation,
the founders of New England were holy men, enshrined
by patriotism as well as piety. The *Nation*'s skepticism or
Bret Harte's Western rebelliousness were still fairly new,
and later kinds of anti-Puritanism unimaginable. New
England was "the seedbed of this great American republic," and as such the pattern for progressive society
everywhere. To a Beecher, the especially important pattern was that set by rural New England, paradoxical as
always, at once democratic and traditional. Here, despite
the rough equality, ministers and other leading citizens
were respected. Within the surviving Congregational order, lively religious and political dispute was taken for
granted. To Emerson, brought up in Boston where most
of the old arguments seemed to be swallowed up in the
new liberalism, the beginning of the nineteenth century

was a dead period without a book or a thought. To Harriet Beecher Stowe, the villages of her youth were "burning like live coals under this obscurity with all the fervid activity of an intense, newly kindled, peculiar, and individual life." These were the coals that burst into blaze in the period of Emerson's own maturity.

Her idea of the founders was based on mythology, living oral tradition, and limited but intense reading, especially of Cotton Mather's *Magnalia Christi Americana,* to which she repeatedly refers. Her version of New England religious history blurs some episodes and skips others, but contains some vivid and correct insights. Knowing something of the earthy side of a preacher's problems, she knew that a society entirely made up of intensely introspective saints would fall apart, and its churches would perish with it. Thus she strongly approved the Halfway Covenant, under which the church was kept in existence by admitting to a halfway status not only the children but also the grandchildren of church members without requiring the definite experience of Divine Grace demanded by Puritan theology. This compromise, the work of the practical second generation of American Puritans, she pushes back to the founding of New England. She also associates it, in Chapter 28, with Cotton Mather himself, who was born in the year the Halfway Covenant was adopted. (It was, however, defended by him and both his father and grandfather had played a part in its adoption.) Lavishing on Mather her highest praise—in Chapter 28 he is "good, motherly Cotton Mather" and in Chapter 19 he has already been called a "delightful New England grandmother"—she laments that Edwards undid his maternal work, throwing out of the church the children of the saints and demanding, as the condition of readmission, an experience of regeneration which one could do nothing to earn.

When Mrs. Stowe dealt with Edwards, she was dealing with a subject she understood more deeply than she did the earlier history of New England religion. She was no intellectual, and did not concern herself with Edwards' awesome metaphysical system. His theology, however, was the background of her father's and her husband's careers, and furnished the terms for the most severe inner conflicts of her life. Because she approached Edwards not as an academic student but as a person who had tried to live by his teachings, she understood one thing that has only recently become clear to historians of American religion. Not just because he helped destroy the Halfway Covenant, but for many reasons, Edwards was at least as much an aberration as a culmination in the history of American religion. This is, after all, usually true of religious genius when it appears within an established church.

Modern admirers of Edwards are often affected by Protestant neo-orthodoxy. It is important in understanding Mrs. Stowe's treatment to remember that this approach was not available to her. She and her generation had to confront not neo-orthodoxy, but orthodoxy. Hell was not a metaphysical necessity or an absence from God, but a real place full of real fire, described accurately and not just poetically by preachers of great dramatic talent. In this place oneself and most of the people one loved were probably destined to spend an eternity of torture. To accept this concrete fact as a necessary consequence of the nature of things, and yet to love that nature of things with all one's heart, took a man of Edwards' own spiritual and intellectual gifts. The surprising thing, as Mrs. Stowe fully understood, was not that he had failed to convert all his countrymen to his own austere views—nothing could be more contrary to his own estimate of depraved humanity—but rather that his work had dominated and inspired the religious leaders of a hardheaded community for so long. Some of Mrs. Stowe's generation, looking back in revulsion to their early religious training, were able to dismiss Edwards as a primitive malevolent monster with no relevance to their lives or to reality. However successful this dismissal was for some—and it was seldom entirely successful—Mrs. Stowe could not echo it. The power and beauty of Edwards' system was too much a part of her education, her understanding of parts of his achievement was too acute, and her view of life too close to his own.

Mrs. Stowe knew that Edwards broke up, once and for all, "the crust of formalism and mechanical piety" which had been one inevitable consequence of the compromise arrangement she so much admired in itself. With still greater penetration, she knew that his fearless and uncompromising search for ultimate truth had "sawed the great dam and let out the whole waters of discussion all over New England," and thus given rise even to the pantheistic heresies of Emerson and Parker.[12] She also knew—it was the problem central to her father's career—that the conquest of many of the churches by the New Divinity had driven away large numbers of members. Nobody knew better or from harsher experience the toll taken among the most sensitive by the effort to live up to the impossible. All these consequences of the work of New England's major prophet had to be weighed against each other, and they are so weighed in the superb *obiter dicta* which constitute the chief enduring interest of *Oldtown Folks*.

Both this novel and *The Minister's Wooing*, Mrs. Stowe's other main effort to deal in literature with Edwardsian theology, are still more directly concerned with Edwards' disciples than with their master. As Mrs. Stowe's husband, in a penetrating sketch of her father, points out, President Edwards' writings almost took the place of St.

Paul's for a generation of New England divines, and gave rise to arguments of almost proportionate intensity.[13]

The chief problem of the Edwardsian school of theologians was to bring divine sovereignty and foreknowledge into some sort of relation to human responsibility, and to reconcile both of these with God's benevolence. Like their predecessors for two millennia, they labored to understand the necessity of evil and sin. Why, they asked—never doubting that there was an answer—must most of God's creatures be made in such a way that it was impossible for them to fulfill the duties God had prescribed for them. Facing boldly up to the most sacred mysteries, they asked why the sacrifice of Christ and the whole work of redemption was necessary. Instead of saving a small remnant at this vast price, could not God have saved all by a different sort of creation? The most dangerous way to answer this question, as well as the most profound, is to deny that God's right and wrong are those with which men are familiar. To Edwards, whose ultimate standards according to his modern biographer were aesthetic rather than moralistic, it was enough to say that the scheme was the means of exhibiting God's greatest glory.

Practical preachers, concerned more with preserving the moral order of the community and less with contemplation of ultimate truth, had to search for some less exalted way to demonstrate that the terrible fate awaiting most of mankind made some sort of sense. Joseph Bellamy, whose *True Religion Delineated* ("my grandmother's blue book") is quoted at length and accurately in *Oldtown Folks,* was a didactic simplifier of the Edwardsian system. Nobody is harsher in insisting on man's total depravity and the limitation of Christ's Atonement to the elect. Almost scolding the presumptuous advocates of universal salvation who were already rampant in New England,

Bellamy insists that "the door is not opened wider than Christ desired it should be."[14] Yet he demonstrates, in somewhat Panglossian fashion, that sin and its inevitable consequences are a means of the greatest possible good of the universe; that it is actually better, in terms understandable to us, that the world be as dreadful as it is.

Samuel Hopkins, Edwards' favorite and perhaps his most gifted disciple, is the principal character in Mrs. Stowe's *The Minister's Wooing*. A major systematic theologian, Hopkins is best known—or rather *was* best known when he was known at all—for carrying to a terrifying conclusion Edwards' most compelling doctrine, that all virtue consists in an austere, mystical, completely disinterested love of being in general, and thus ultimately in love of God.[15] To attain this kind of virtue, Hopkins and Edwards agree, human beings need direct and continuous Divine help. Without it all such trivialities as self-love, natural affections, or even good done for the purpose of achieving reward, earthly or heavenly, are evil in God's sight. Hopkins pushes this one step farther. We must, he argues, so love holiness that if our own eternal damnation be a necessary part of God's scheme, we must willingly acquiesce in it. If we cannot meet this test, all is hopeless for us.

This doctrine, and its inevitable corollary that we must also acquiesce willingly in the damnation of others, is represented in *Oldtown Folks* by another major New England theologian, who plays a recurrent and important part in the novel, this time in disguise, as "Dr. Stern." Dr. Stern is Nathaniel Emmons, a follower of Hopkins and a dry and dull theologian, but the most extraordinary specimen of the Calvinist personality ever developed in the historic seedbed.[16]

Emmons' theological system, indefatigably worked

out over a long life, was a variant of Hopkins' and need not concern us much. With almost none of Edwards' metaphysical interest, Emmons insisted on crystal-clear logic and specialized in pushing the Edwardsian paradoxes to an almost perverse extreme. He took an extreme view of Divine agency in regeneration, and held firmly to complete individual moral responsibility. A moral activist, he taught that regeneration was shown through a series of moral exercises, not general inclination or taste. Though God was completely sovereign, He was yet limited by the categories of right and wrong, whose nature we were able correctly to perceive through intuition. (Here Emmons, like most of his contemporaries, was influenced by the Scottish commonsense philosophers.) Underlying these paradoxes was the fundamental contradiction common to the post-Edwards school: God was an utterly unlimited ruler; yet his opinions and conduct were laid down for Him in detail by His humble creature, Nathaniel Emmons.

Nowhere does Emmons discuss God's purposes in more excruciating detail than in his many funeral sermons. Always addressing the bereaved directly, as Parson Lothrop does at the funeral in *Oldtown Folks*, Emmons was wont to outline the many ways in which God might have intended the bereavement for their good. If, as was often the case, the deceased had made no profession of religion and might well be damned, God's purpose in so decreeing was laid down all the more scrupulously. The sermon of Dr. Stern's quoted in *Oldtown Folks* is a real one, and its severity is if anything understated by the quotations Mrs. Stowe has chosen.[17] If the saved are not willing properly to enjoy the sufferings of the damned, this proves that they do not really want to go to heaven, or have an incorrect conception of it. "How must Moses feel in seeing Pharaoh! How

must Paul feel in seeing Pilate! How must parents feel
in seeing children, and children in seeing parents, and
friends in seeing friends, separated from them, and
doomed to unutterable and unending misery! What
gratitude must the happy ones feel, and how sincerely
will they praise God for his sovereign and distinguishing
mercy?"[18]

This reference to children was particularly telling,
since as Emmons once pointed out in a child's funeral
sermon, few families failed to experience the loss of a
child.[19] Having described, with feeling, the sufferings
occasioned by such losses, Emmons went on in his usual
systematic fashion to list eight ways in which God might
intend such deaths to work to the edification of the bereaved parents and the eternal advantage of mankind.

It is tempting to us, and it must have been still more
tempting to Mrs. Stowe, to make Emmons simply an
unfeeling monster. She knew, however, that this would
be completely false. Personally kind and compassionate,
Emmons was revered, even perhaps loved, by his long
succession of theological students. He was also particularly in demand as a funeral preacher and, in his strange
uncompromising way, comforter of the bereaved. His
congregation knew that his view of death and the proper attitude toward it by no means rested on his logic-
chopping theology alone. Mrs. Stowe mentions Dr.
Stern's "most affecting autobiography," and Emmons'
own memoir indeed deserves quotation at length. In his
"domestic concerns" Emmons "experienced uncommon
favors and uncommon frowns of providence." Marrying
early a young woman to whom he was deeply devoted,
he became the father of two sons. His wife however fell
into a decline after the birth of the second and shortly
died. Emmons undertook the care of the two children,
whom he "loved to excess." He was forced helplessly to

watch one after the other die of dysentery, in convulsions
and "extreme agonies."

> It is impossible to describe what I felt. I stood a few
> moments, and viewed the remains of my two darlings, who
> had gone to their mother and to their long home, never to
> return. But I soon found the scene too distressing and re-
> tired to my chamber, to meditate in silence upon my forlorn
> condition. I thought there was no sorrow like unto my sor-
> row. I thought my burden was greater than I could bear.
> I felt as though I could not submit to such a complicated
> affliction. My heart rose in all its strength against the gov-
> ernment of God, and then suddenly sunk under its distress,
> which greatly alarmed me. I sprang up, and said to myself,
> I am going into immediate distraction; I must submit, or I
> am undone for ever. In a very few minutes my burden was
> removed, and I felt entirely calm and resigned to the will
> of God. I soon went down, attended to my family concerns,
> and gave directions respecting the interment of my chil-
> dren. I never enjoyed greater happiness in the course of
> my life, than I did all that day and the next. My mind was
> wholly detached from the world, and altogether employed
> in pleasing contemplation of God and divine things. I felt
> as though I could follow my wife and children into eternity,
> with peculiar satisfaction.[20]

Like many another widowed New England minister,
Emmons married twice more. In due time he became
the father of six more children. He had been taught a
lesson, however, and "never indulged such high hopes
concerning my present family, as I presumptuously indulged with respect to the family I have laid in the dust.
I have likewise learned, by past painful experience, to
mourn with those who mourn, and to weep with those
who weep."[21] He had learned particularly, he said, to
follow the mourners from the funeral to their dwellings,

where they sat alone, and to try to bring them some of the consolation which he had himself experienced in his worst trial. In his old age he preached funeral sermons over two of his own children by his second marriage, expressing his own grief but steadfastly setting forth the will of God in these events for the edification of his hearers.

Emmons lived to be ninety-five, conceding nothing to changing times, maintaining a spiritual monopoly of the village of Franklin (in *Oldtown Folks*, "Adams") against Unitarians, Arminians, and all challengers; and even wearing to the end the ancient clerical costume of cocked hat and buckled shoes. In his ninety-first year, on his first visit to New York City, he made the dramatic contribution to the antislavery cause which is briefly described in the novel.

This was the supreme example of the Calvinist pattern of improving the lessons taught by God in death, and this was the pattern which was to be set before the Beecher family in a very special way.

The Calvinist theologian who most influenced Harriet Beecher's upbringing was, of course, Lyman Beecher ("Mr. Avery" in the novel).[22] Beecher was no Emmons. Indeed, if he had been, his daughter's life might have been easier; she would either have been compelled into submission or driven into outright revolt. Beecher was one of the principal adapters of the Calvinist heritage to the nineteenth century, and his career marks a sort of halfway house between the austere religion of Edwards and the sentimental, anti-intellectual liberalism of his son Henry Ward Beecher.

As a theologian, Lyman Beecher was not especially interesting or profound. He followed the more liberal branch of the Edwards school, through the influence of his teacher, President Timothy Dwight of Yale, and his close friend Nathaniel Taylor. Taylor, like Beecher, knew that in the democratic and pluralistic age in which he lived Calvinism could survive only if its moral soundness could be demonstrated in terms acceptable to many. Thus sin, to Taylor, was not as it was to Bellamy and Hopkins and Emmons, a means deliberately chosen by God, in preference to other possibilities, as the best way of carrying out His plan. It was instead unpreventable in the nature of things: even God could not choose human freedom without including freedom to do evil. Taylor's favorite formula for explaining what was left of predestination was that man's propensity to do evil amounted to "certainty with power to the contrary." His motto was "Follow Truth if it carries you over Niagara."

Beecher followed Taylor in these theoretical matters. His own great role was not that of theologian but that of a preacher, revivalist, and above all fighter. His successive fights, however, amounted in the long run to a compromise, since his enemies were successively infidels (meaning eighteenth-century Deists), Episcopalians, Unitarians, ultrarevivalists, and finally, and most bitterly, ultraorthodox Calvinists. He also campaigned fervently against Sabbath-breaking, duelling, and (after giving up the genial practices described in the Cloudland consociation meeting in the novel) drink. Thus Beecher played a major part in opening the doors of New England religion to emotionalism, moralism, and reform. Yet in his own mind he remained loyal to Edwards, Dwight, and Bellamy.

Above all, as Beecher's fascinating autobiography reveals, he was a man of superlative vigor and gusto, who kept a gun beside him to shoot birds if any flew over while he was writing a sermon, delighted in fishing or roughhousing with his boys, wept over Scott and (with regret for the poet's failings) over Byron, and even, in private, played the fiddle and danced out of sheer exuberance. As a father, he was unbearably demanding. The colorful and lively center of the household, a pattern for affectionate emulation by his children, he of course insisted like his contemporaries on instant obedience, drastically enforced once and for all and then taken for granted. In dealing with his children's souls, his views made outright coercion impossible. Leaving them free to accept or reject Divine Grace, all-important and freely offered, he watched indefatigably with them for signs of a changing heart, and once he found such signs played his children like the skilled professional fisher of souls he was, alternating pulling them in and slackening the line, but never letting them off the hook.

The results were impressive. Of Beecher's children four were preachers, and at least three of these achieved wide public notice. One child became a college president, one an important female educator, and one an immensely influential author and the uncrowned queen of Anglo-American evangelical antislavery reform. Rather surprisingly, only one—or possibly two—committed suicide. But all the ministerial sons and all but one of the daughters eventually rejected even the loose kind of orthodoxy represented by their father. Some of them wandered far indeed. (One daughter, Isabella, eventually became convinced that she herself was destined to be the new Messiah, an equal partner with Jesus Christ.) Of them all, the closest to Harriet was Henry, whose gushy religion of unlimited hope and undiscriminating love becomes more understandable when one sees it against the background of Edwards, Emmons, and Lyman Beecher.[23]

Harriet Beecher was brought up in Litchfield, Connecticut, and in Edwardsian Calvinism as taught and modified by her father. According to a contemporary biographer she had committed to memory twenty-seven hymns and two long chapters of the Bible by the time she was four.[24] An early alternative to her father's Presbyterianism was furnished by the Episcopalianism of her mother's family, and visits to "Nutplains," the house of her mother's cultivated and comparatively easy-going family, were among her most pleasant childhood recollections.

The most important part of her religious education was, however, that provided by death, which visited the Beecher family as often as it did most large families of the day. The first important disaster of her childhood was the death of her mother, Lyman Beecher's first wife, Roxana. From every record a simple, saintly, and beautiful woman, Roxana, mourned tempestuously but with real and deep grief by Lyman, became a sort of ethereal cult figure to the Beecher children. Henry Ward, who was two when she died, said that his feeling for her was comparable to that of a devout Catholic for the Virgin Mary.[25] To Harriet she formed the pattern for an angelic mother dying in her offspring's early childhood, a figure that recurs in her novels, among them *Oldtown Folks*. There were of course other family tragedies, but the one which circumstances made most crucial was that of a young man Harriet herself probably barely knew, Alexander Metcalf Fisher. Death, Emmons had said in sermon after sermon, should be sanctified to the living. In a statement which unconsciously echoed this doctrine, Mrs. Stowe's son and grandson said a long time later that Fisher's death provided "an epoch in the history of the Beecher family, and in the history of the New England theology." After this episode, they said, even Lyman Beecher's serenity may never have recovered, but without it, at least one novel of Mrs. Stowe's and at least one important heretical work of Edward Beecher's would never have been written.[26]

Fisher, a youthful prodigy, was named adjunct professor of mathematics and natural philosophy at Yale at twenty-three. He fell in love with Catharine Beecher, the most vivacious and one of the most gifted of the Beecher children. Since he was a young man of great promise, impeccable morals, and sound religion (though his efforts to receive assurance of saving Grace were as yet unrewarded) he was more than acceptable to Catharine's father. In 1822 Fisher said good-bye to his fiancée for a brief professional trip to England. It became Lyman Beecher's duty to tell his daughter that the ship *Albion,* with Fisher aboard, had sunk off the Irish coast.

Lyman Beecher, like any Calvinist ministerial father, did his very best to see that this loss was sanctified to his daughter. He could not, however, depart from his life's teachings and his idea of plain honesty enough to tell her that the young man was in Heaven. In a long series of tender, considerate letters he tried to persuade her of the justice of God's ways and her duty, whatever Fisher's eternal destiny, to turn this grief to her own spiritual advantage. In her long, agonized, and spirited answers to her father's letters Catharine declared herself unable willingly to accept the possible damnation of her impeccably virtuous fiancé.[27]

On a visit to Fisher's family, Catharine found in his papers evidence of his unsuccessful struggle for assurance of salvation, which seemed to rivet his fate. And since the village the Fisher family lived in was Franklin, Fisher's funeral sermon was preached by no lesser figure than Nathaniel Emmons. It was as mild as any Emmons sermon.[28] The preacher pictured graphically the anguish of the ship's company, but devoted most of his time to an abstract demonstration of "Divine Sovereignty in the Death of Men." He ended with a great deal of praise of Fisher, and even, stretching a point farther than Beecher had, suggested that "Though he never professed, yet there is some ground to hope that he had experienced a saving change." Either way, of course, it was necessary for his father and friends to learn the lesson taught by the death of this excellent young man, and Emmons particularly hoped that "It may have a happy effect upon a very sensible and highly accomplished young lady, who may imagine she has the largest share of affliction in this instance of mortality."

In a sense Emmons' hope that Fisher's death might be improved to Catharine's advantage was fulfilled, but the ways of Providence are more inscrutable than he realized, and things hardly turned out as he could have wished. Catharine, as her letters make clear, listened patiently and at length to Emmons' preaching and her father's pleas, and by both was gradually persuaded not to accept but to reject the whole Calvinist scheme. In a long series of able arguments she denied that God requires of us anything He does not give the ability to perform. (One essay was considered by some competent theologians the ablest refutation of Edwards on the Will.)[29] She later contrasted the entire Augustinian system with what she considered the system of common sense, and was even capable, in a letter, of a prim New England blasphemy: "I must have *proof* that all this horrible misery and wrong resulting from the wrong construction or nature of mind is not attributable to the Creator of All Things. His mere word is nothing from the Author of a system which is all ruined and worse than good for nothing. He must clear his character before he can offer me a Revelation!"[30]

The main result of her departure from her ancestral religion was still more in a New England vein. She became convinced that mankind can be made perfect if, and only if, a sufficiently intense effort is made on behalf of education. Catharine Beecher therefore became a

school principal, and later a tireless, belligerent pro-
moter of education in general, particularly for women
and for the West. In the first stage of this career, desiring
a wider sphere of usefulness as part of her recovery from
Fisher's death, she established a school at Hartford,
where her sister Harriet joined her, as an apprentice
teacher, in 1824.

It was in Hartford, in close consultation with Catharine and, by letter, with her far more heretical brother
Edward, that Harriet Beecher underwent her own two
successive experiences of conversion. The first was conventional in everything except its ease. Hearing her father preach, on a "dewey, fresh summer morning"
during her first vacation, she became ecstatically convinced that she had the friend she needed, and told her
father that she had given herself to Jesus, and he had
taken her. "Is it so?" he said, holding me silently to his
heart, as I felt the hot tears fall on my head. 'Then has
a new flower blossomed in the kingdom this day.' "[31]

But Lyman Beecher's religion was not yet Henry
Ward Beecher's, and hot tears and blossoms were only
a small part of it. Instances of delusions of conversion
were many and familiar, and he felt obliged to question
her further about her willingness to be alone in the universe with God, and her acceptance of her own possible
sin and misery. She went back to Hartford full of doubts,
and argued them out painfully with Catharine and, by
letter, with Edward. She was afraid that her own actions
rose too much from a wish to be loved, but, like Catharine, found it more and more difficult to understand how
God could have required heights of virtue which he had
purposely made people unable to obtain. By 1830, however, she again thought she had reached a certainty of
happiness and rest in the love of Christ.[32] This certainty,
as far as we can tell, she never quite lost and never
securely held.

In her mature life Harriet Beecher was to see clearly, as she repeatedly indicates in the novel before us, that Edwardsian Calvinism of the Emmons variety drove the majority into religious indifference, the most courageous minority into active hostility, and the most sensitive minority into hell on earth. Yet she was far too close to her father and his religion, and too deeply convinced about the faithfulness of Calvinist pessimism to actual life, to abandon the inherited doctrine soon, easily, or ever completely. Essentially brave and intelligent, introspective, given to emotional storms in the Victorian manner but not without a good deal of hardness and egotism, she was forced increasingly to give up the search for complete understanding of God's ways. According to her own repeated statements, she was able to conclude, in the worst crisis of her life, that the mystery of God's dealing with men was swallowed up in the greater mystery of the love of Christ.[33] To the extent that she really achieved this conviction, she was surely a better Christian, and perhaps even a better Christian theologian, than Nathaniel Emmons. The genuineness of her somewhat insistent serenity is beyond our search and essentially irrelevant to our purpose. What is certain is that her inner experience was sufficiently rich and intense to give rise to the best of her writing.

As much as any Beecher, Harriet Beecher Stowe during the time of her own struggles felt called to minister to the spiritual needs of others. Though she wrote hymns and called some of her essays sermons, convention barred her from the pulpit and opened the way, not without some shaking of heads, to ladylike literary work. Furthermore, as the wife of a distinguished but impractical theologian and soon enough the mother of a struggling family, she felt the need to supplement the family income. From about 1840 Mrs. Stowe's life centered, at least on a worldly level, in a literary career. Yet this career itself could never be separated entirely from her spiritual Pilgrim's Progress and the many severe personal trials still in store. We must now consider at once her inner and her outer life, in the period when both were leading toward *Oldtown Folks*.[34]

Mrs. Stowe's early sketches, written while her father was president of Lane Seminary in Cincinnati, exploit her nostalgic feeling for the New England scene and do not venture into religion or theology beyond a few platitudes. *Uncle Tom's Cabin*, however, was written like most of her best books at a time of personal crisis and therefore plunged deeper. Once more God's mysterious ways had been exhibited in death, this time in her loss by cholera of a small son. *Uncle Tom*, written in the midst of poverty and the distractions of housekeeping, much of it nonetheless in a state of religious exaltation, is haunted by the deaths of children. Sometimes, as in the case of Little Eva, these deaths are models of holy and happy death reminiscent of thousands of contemporary tracts. Sometimes, however, they are grim and terrible. The slave Prue, who laconically reports the death of her own child as a result of her mistress's cruelty and neglect, is absolutely unsentimentalized. Prue knows that she is ugly, and wicked, and supposes she is going to torment; but she is so miserable here and now that she does not care.

Much of the overt religious content of *Uncle Tom's Cabin* is in the tearful revivalistic vein which had, with the partial support of Lyman Beecher, become increasingly dominant in American Christianity. But the mark of Calvinism is there in the harsh realism about human nature that gives the book its lasting bite. Only Eva and Uncle Tom are capable of any dependable goodness. For less favored characters, the book again and again makes clear, "temptations to hardheartedness . . . always overcome frail human nature when the prospect of sudden and rapid gain is weighed in the balance, with no heavier counterpoise than the interests of the helpless and unprotected."[35]

After Uncle Tom, Mrs. Stowe's name became, in Annie Fields's phrase, "A sacred talisman, especially in Old and New England,"[36] and the great author set off on a triumphal tour of Old England and Europe. Like most American authors, Mrs. Stowe found Europe somewhat overwhelming. She was fussed over by duchesses, and never quite got over making inept references to aristocratic glamour. (There are a few in *Oldtown Folks,* more in some of her other novels.) Dutifully doing the galleries, she set down her impressions in her travel journal, which is a mixture of conventional rhapsody, extreme provincial naïveté, and shrewd observation. At her shrewdest, she compared art critics to practitioners of the science she knew best and drew a characteristic conclusion. "Divided into little cliques, each with his shibboleth, artists excommunicate each other as heartily as theologians, and a neophyte who should attempt to make up a judgment by their help would be obliged to shift opinions with every circle. I therefore look with my own eyes, for if not the best that might be, they are the best that God has given me."[37]

For a Beecher recording her impressions of Europe, however, other issues were involved than those of aesthetics, issues which could not be so easily dismissed. Defending her ancestral loyalties against Europe's powerful blandishments, Mrs. Stowe harked back dutifully to the oppressions of feudalism and the horrors of the Inquisition. Unlike many American tourists, however, she remembered that slavery was a blemish on New World institutions which might well qualify any con-

tempt for other countries.[38] Despite herself, she was attracted by the majestic ceremonial and uncontroversial
preaching she encountered in the Church of England,
and, still more, by the color and drama of continental
Catholicism. Putting the question "if we *could*, would we
efface from the world such cathedrals as Strasbourg and
Cologne," she answered it easily enough in the negative.[39] Like many Protestant voyagers, she wondered
whether Puritanism's hostility to art and enjoyment was
necessary to religious truth, and she even found something innocent and attractive in the French Sunday. In
Scotland, however, she was recalled to her usual sen-
timents by encountering again Sabbatarianism and
doctrinal preaching. She reminded herself that only
Protestant countries had achieved republican government and that unfortunately, "as a country is free and
self-governed it has fewer public amusements. America
and Scotland have the fewest of any, and Italy the
most."[40] (Both these last two judgments are repeated in
passing in *Oldtown Folks*.)

Finally, musing in Switzerland about the strength and
weaknesses of the Genevan system and of Calvinism in
general, giving due weight to the burning of Servetus
and the Salem witchcraft trials, she reiterated her firm,
if ambivalent loyalty:

> Calvinism, in its essential features, will never cease from
> the earth, because the great fundamental facts of nature
> are Calvinistic, and men with strong minds and wills always
> discover it. The predestination of a sovereign will is written
> over all things. The old Greek tragedians read it, and ex-
> pressed it. So did Mahomet, Napoleon, Cromwell. Why?
> They found it so by their own experience; they tried the
> forces of nature enough to find their strength ... To him
> who strives in vain with the giant forces of evil, what calm
> in the thought of an overpowering will, so that will be

crowned by goodness! However grim, to the distrusting, looks this fortress of sovereignty in times of flowery ease, yet in times when 'the waters roar and are troubled, and the mountains shake with the swelling thereof,' it has always been the refuge of God's people. All this I say, while I fully sympathize with the causes which incline many fine and beautiful minds against the system.[41]

This conclusion was shortly to be tested again by a further shaking of Harriet's foundations. After completing, in 1856, her second antislavery novel, *Dred*, which contained a strong attack on ministers lukewarm to the cause, as her father had been, she was turned sharply back to the problem that had always haunted her most deeply. In 1857 her favorite son Henry was drowned at Dartmouth in a swimming accident. Not only was she almost overwhelmed with grief; all the old questions were again raised, and they were still theological questions. Not without difficulty, with the help of Catharine among others of her family, she managed to settle in her mind the question of Henry's eternal state. In one desperate letter she hinted that God could not be so unfair as to punish one who was not only innocent but "the child of one who had trusted and confided in him for years."[42] She really knew, however, that this was pushing the idea of a hereditary covenant too far, and it was in the same letter that she was able to make the statement, quoted earlier, that Christ's love must swallow up the mystery of God's ways with us.[43] Nevertheless, neither then nor later was this an easy conclusion for Mrs. Stowe to reach and hold, and it was in part her renewed pondering of the problem that sent her back to ancestral ground for her novels. From this point on, her main overt subject was what her main implied subject had always been, God's ways and New England's perception of them.

In 1858, asked for a contribution to the first issue of the *Atlantic Monthly,* that organ of Boston Unitarianism and uplift, Mrs. Stowe sent in, incongruously enough, a parable of death as teacher in the traditional orthodox mold, only slightly softened. A father, sending a package of presents from town to his cheerful family, includes a black mourning veil. Most of the children think it ugly, but a minister who turns up says that until one has seen the world through such a veil, he has not truly lived. Sure enough, family catastrophe provides an opportunity for its use, and the sketch ends with the mother, who has lost a child, putting away the veil with her sad mementoes "in solemn thankfulness." Sentimental as it may seem, this story is much more succinct and effective than the great bulk of Mrs. Stowe's potboiling occasional pieces.[44]

Her next contribution to the *Atlantic* was a review article about the first two volumes of that delightful mine of American clerical lore, W. B. Sprague's *Annals of the American Pulpit.* Not only does she demonstrate by affectionate retelling of Sprague's anecdotes the provincial eccentricity of New England ministers over two centuries, she also emphasizes their unrelenting and courageous search for complete, logical answers to the most difficult questions. Increasingly free herself from the need to struggle with the particular formulations of New England theology, she insists (doubtless with some *Atlantic* authors in mind) that "It is a mark of a shallow mind to scorn these theological wrestlings and surgings; they have had in them something even sublime."[45] Mrs. Stowe was a thrifty author, and she was to incorporate a large section of this excellent essay verbatim into Chapter 19 of *Oldtown Folks.*

In 1859 Mrs. Stowe published *The Minister's Wooing,* which prefigures *Oldtown Folks* more completely than any of her other works. The book's main character is Samuel Hopkins, and Mrs. Stowe had done some historical research. Her main, though not her only, source of information was Edwards Amasa Park, the last major developer and defender of Edwardsian theology. Park had written a useful biography of Hopkins and was working on one of Emmons which was to be still better. Since he taught at Andover Seminary, whose faculty Calvin Stowe had recently joined, Mrs. Stowe was able to read him parts of her manuscript. As a novelist may, she took her historical research lightly, and altered to fit her plot the incidents of Hopkins' life. For this she was criticized by orthodox reviewers. Yet her liberties with Hopkins' doctrines were few, and her attitude toward them far from completely hostile.

One subplot of the book is concerned with Hopkins' brave and early (and actual) denunciation of slavery. The major plot is a recapitulation of the loss of Fisher, seen through Mrs. Stowe's own mourning veil. The fiancé of a devoted Puritan maiden is drowned at sea, or seems to be (the fact that he turns up later is an unimportant concession to public taste). The girl, a saintly character modeled not on Catharine but on Mrs. Stowe's mother, Roxana Beecher,[46] accepts the loss in the proper spirit, but the boy's mother is unable to do so. Like Catharine, and perhaps a little like Mrs. Stowe herself, the bereaved mother goes most convincingly through torments of despair and near-blasphemy, only to be saved in the end, rather unconvincingly, by the simple heart-religion of a Negro slave.

The Minister's Wooing has its share of gush and melodrama and conventional piety, and is further marred by the introduction of a stock French countess, doubtless to show the author's ability to handle a high European style. Yet in at least two chapters the author anticipates and equals the best of *Oldtown Folks*. Chapter 4, "Theological Tea," develops successfully the new genre of dialect folk theology. And the first part of Chapter 24, "Views of Divine Government," is Mrs. Stowe's most direct and most powerful piece of theological criticism so far. Grand and impressive as the New England systems are, she is now sure that they differ from the New Testament "as the living embrace of a friend does from his lifeless body, mapped out under the knife of the anatomical demonstrator." "All systems," moreover, "that deal with the infinite are, besides, exposed to danger from small, unsuspected admixtures of human error, which become deadly when carried to such vast results."[47] Deadly, that is, to the most sensitive spirits, who take them most to heart in the concerns of life and death.

Attacked by the orthodox, Mrs. Stowe was reassured by Lowell, who not only praised her for going back to ground she knew but, as somebody who himself had to confess "a strong sympathy with many parts of Calvinist orthodoxy," gave her his own rather odd theological imprimatur: "If, with your heart and brain, you are not orthodox, in Heaven's name, who is? If you mean 'Calvinistic,' no woman could ever be such, for Calvinism is logic, and no woman worth the name could ever live by syllogisms."[48]

In 1862 Mrs. Stowe published another New England novel, *The Pearl of Orr's Island*. This was again a half-success, and was less directly concerned with theology than *The Minister's Wooing*. Her other work of the same year, *Agnes of Sorrento*, transferred the familiar theological issues with no great success to Renaissance Italy. It was time for her to bring her favorite theme and her favorite locale back together, and she was now ready to do so.

Through the sixties, through the strains of the Civil

War (in which Mrs. Stowe called for the destruction of the ungodly as fiercely as any Old Testament prophet), through the drudgery of prolific professional authorship, through the difficulties of emerging into a grander style of living, Mrs. Stowe was brooding over her major New England novel, and in her own phrase "skimming and saving the cream" for it.[49] By 1865 she was ready to start the actual writing of it. With her religious and literary development in mind, it is possible for us to see clearly some of the many sources on which she drew.

Once more, a major work coincided with a major grief, this time the destruction by alcoholism of her son Fred.[50] She was by now, however, accustomed to grief, and there is no evidence that this disaster hit her as hard as Henry's death had. *Oldtown Folks* does not, like *The Minister's Wooing*, show the effects of obsession with a particular loss, though the general problem of accepting whatever is Divinely ordained is constantly present to its Calvinist characters, and several of Mrs. Stowe's past griefs are occasionally reflected. For some years she had been tending more and more toward something like her mother's religion of accepting, unanalytic love. Increasingly, she was finding the Protestant Episcopal Church the proper vessel for this kind of piety. To Mrs. Stowe, and to many other New Englanders of her generation, Anglicanism seemed to offer far more than ritual and decorum. There was, as Ellery Davenport points out in *Oldtown Folks*, plenty of Calvinism in the Thirty-Nine Articles. There was also, however, confession and absolution in the service, and the assurance, which former Edwardsians badly needed, that God hates nothing he has made. Yet Mrs. Stowe still retained a certain detachment, and was able in *Oldtown Folks* to make fun of the more extreme claims of the Church of England in Revolutionary America.[51]

More than ever before, she was attracted at the end of the fifties by her father's archenemy, Bostonian liberalism, especially in the person of its reigning favorite, Dr. Oliver Wendell Holmes. Understandably, Holmes had been a little worried when in 1859 he had been deputed to escort the Stowes to a meeting of the Saturday Club. The teetotal and straitlaced Stowes were indeed gently baited by the discreetly jocular assembly, and Holmes hoped that Mrs. Stowe would not disapprove of him *very* much.[52]

Holmes was worried about more fundamental matters than the wine and wit of the Saturday Club. Like Mrs. Stowe, he was the son of a moderate Calvinist minister, but he had reacted against his upbringing far more strongly. In his *Autocrat,* and still more in its sequel *The Professor at the Breakfast Table,* he was unable to resist baiting the orthodox, urbanely but none the less sharply. His article on Jonathan Edwards was an eloquent version of the usual liberal caricature. And his lectures are full of his own bland synthesis of uplift, relativism, mechanism, and the ethics of the New Testament—a system at least as full of paradox as that of Nathaniel Emmons.[53]

Mrs. Stowe, however, answered Holmes' letter with great cordiality and some sprightliness, and he became her closest literary friend. Both the Stowes defended Holmes against the attacks of the orthodox when in 1861 he published his novel *Elsie Venner,* an odd parable of determinism and moral irresponsibility in which the heroine's character is shaped by a prenatal rattlesnake bite.[54] As both Holmes and Mrs. Stowe realized, both were struggling with the same upbringing, and neither was completely victorious in the struggle. "I have been," said Holmes

in the doctrinal boiler at Andover, and the rational ice-chest at Cambridge. I have been hung with my head downwards, from the hook of a theological dogma, and set on my feet again by the hand of uninspired common-sense. I have found myself like a nursery-tree, growing up with labels of this and that article of faith wired to my limbs. The labels have dropped off, but the wires are only buried in my flesh, which has grown over them ... I do not say that you have been through all this ... Yet, I say we have had some experiences in common, and however imperfectly I express myself by word or by letter, now or at any time, there are mental and emotional states which you can understand as none can do who have not been through the chronometer of experience.[55]

I do not believe you or I can ever get the iron of Calvinism out of our souls.[56]

More than Holmes was quite able to realize, this was true of Mrs. Stowe, and there is one indication that, despite her cordiality, she was stung by his constant belaboring of the orthodox. Identifying herself fully, for the first time in a long while, with her father's people rather than with his Bostonian enemies, she wrote Fields refusing to have *Oldtown Folks* published in the *Atlantic:*

There are several objections to the plan you propose. In the first place, as to the success of the book *as* a book. It is more to me than a story; it is my resume of the whole spirit and body of New England—a country that now is exerting such an influence on the civilized world that to know it truly becomes an object.

But the Atlantic has on the part of *my* people (i.e., the orthodox) prejudices to encounter that would *predispose* them to look suspiciously on it, more than ever by the fact of its being by a Beecher.

Dr. Holmes has stung and irritated them by his sharp, scathing irony and keen ridicule; and, after all, they are not ridiculous, and the estimate of New England life and principles and orthodoxy, as dramatically set forth, must be graver and wider than he has revealed it.

Under all the drollery that is to be found in it, this book will be found to have in it the depths of the most solemn tragedy of life, and I shall make it my means of saying many things which I hope will be accepted pacifically on all sides. It will answer my purpose better to be read at once in a book. To spend two years in getting my story before the world, before half of my friends will read or judge, would not suit my views.[57]

By the sixties, Mrs. Stowe was indeed ready to write about all the varieties of New England religious experience: agnosticism, Episcopalianism, Arminianism, and various shades of orthodoxy, with remarkable detachment. It is worth noticing however that the variety that comes off worst, despite the personal worth of its representative, is Parson Lothrop's Arminianism. This kind of liberal optimism, the ancestor of Holmes' Brahminism, proves inadequate to deal with death, and that is still for Mrs. Stowe the main test. Even Ellery Davenport, the scoffer, is allowed to speak more convincingly than the liberal Christian optimist.

One major remaining source both for Mrs. Stowe's opinions and her facts, and one whose importance is often minimized, was the author's husband. Professor Calvin Stowe, by no means the hen-pecked mediocrity he is sometimes turned into (even by his wife), accepted with a good deal of grace the difficult role of attendant to a literary lioness. A man of considerable Biblical learning (he was so fond of Hebrew studies that Mrs. Stowe referred to him as "My old Rab," for Rabbi), he remained more definitely than his wife a follower of Edwards. Yet, like her and like many of the most intelligent members of his generation, he hung onto his loyalties with difficulty. In letters to his father-in-law, he expressed his tormenting doubts about God and Christ, and his concern over his own sensual tendencies.[58] Outwardly serene enough, he had a reputation as a narrator in New England dialect of odd incidents from his boyhood in Natick, Massachusetts. These formed the main basis of incident and minor character in *Oldtown Folks,* and Calvin Stowe was permitted to criticize the manuscript as it was written.

The most surprising fact about Calvin Stowe is that he saw visions, strange appearances he had learned to take for granted, sometimes a man and woman, sometimes a boy, sometimes vague cloudy shapes. He was also occasionally visited by clairvoyant intuitions about death and the dead. From time to time Mrs. Stowe, partly because of her husband's gift but more out of her own griefs, gave serious consideration to spiritualism. In the long run, however, she largely rejected it. Edwards, after all, had had no use for visions, and Dr. Park of Andover was sure Calvin Stowe's visions came from a disease of the optic nerve.[59] Nonetheless, the visions were included in *Oldtown Folks* with the rest of Calvin Stowe's memories, and were the part of the book which occasioned the most contemporary discussion. To later readers, it seems probable that the author was not much more interested in them than we are.

With her husband's reminiscences, Mrs. Stowe mixed episodes from her own childhood and her father's, incidents already used in her earlier works, and items drawn from research. This eclecticism, besides providing harmless work for the literary detective, seems to raise some doubt not only about the authenticity but about the dating of Mrs. Stowe's principal account of New England society. Pointers scattered through the text of *Oldtown Folks*—mentions of the Constitutional Convention, then of Washington as President, then of the French Revolution and the Terror—date the story precisely; it takes place in the years from 1787 to 1793. For the book's most important purposes, it does not matter a great deal that some of its incidents occurred in the Beecher family twenty and thirty years later. Its main subject is the twilight of New England's Calvinist order. That order declined over a long period, and at a different pace in different places. Mrs. Stowe knew this decline both at first hand and through her father's reminiscences. Her own life extended from 1811 almost until the end of the century. More important, by the time she wrote *Oldtown Folks,* her immediate and acute experience ran from Nathaniel Emmons to Oliver Wendell Holmes.

For whatever it is worth, many of the book's particular incidents and characters have long been assigned real antecedents, and we can assign a few more. Local tradition, alive in the time of Mrs. Stowe's early biographers, identified many of the minor *Oldtown* characters.[60] Parson Lothrop, whose real name was Stephen Badger, was an Arminian, avoided doctrinal preaching, and modeled his style on that of Addison.[61] Parson Badger did have a wife whose Tory sympathies were tolerated as the eccentricity of a great lady. Uncle Fly is modeled on a Natick tavernkeeper, and Sam Lawson on a real village character named Sam Lawton. The narrator's jovial Harvard uncle is William Bigelow, a real "Uncle Bill" of Calvin Stowe's and a Natick wit and occasional poet. Mrs. Stowe herself refers her readers to a source for the town's haunted house and the legend of Sir Harry Frankland that explains the haunting.[62] The book's Indians have actual counterparts even to their names. Natick was founded in 1651 as a refuge for John Eliot's "praying Indians," and only Indians were at first permitted to own land there. As the American story so often goes, by 1750 most of the land was in white hands, and the Indians hung on as a sort of ragged fringe on village society. The details of daily life in Oldtown—food, clothes, speech, and so forth—are no doubt part of both Stowes' common memories of their separate upbringings. A few such details are apparently drawn from Lyman Beecher's reminiscences of a still earlier time.[63]

Of the three child characters on whom the plot is loosely hung, Horace Holyoke, the useful but colorless narrator, is of course poor Calvin Stowe himself. Tina is Mrs. Stowe's liveliest child, her daughter Georgiana. As for Harry, with his ringlets and his ineffable smile, if he is anybody he is little Eva, with perhaps some echoes, when he is patiently enduring affliction and defending only his religion, of Uncle Tom. This religion, which combines a remarkable certainty of God's love with a strong taste for Episcopalian formulations, is that of Roxana Beecher and her earlier literary incarnations. It is the kind of religion for which Mrs. Stowe herself had struggled all her life with only partial success.

Miss Rossiter manages, as Mrs. Stowe was trying to do, to move from Calvinism through doubt to a religion of love. But her younger sister Emily is, like Catharine Beecher, unable to recover from exposure to Dr. Stern's (Emmons') "appalling doctrines," made still more devastating by the loss of a favorite brother (not a fiancé). Instead of becoming a heretic like Catharine, Emily takes the road to moral ruin. The story is told in the exchange of letters between the Rossiter brother and sister, with the brother concluding that the family had done wrong to allow Emily to be "baited and tortured with ultra-Calvinism."

The supreme example of this kind of ultra-Calvinism is Dr. Stern, who haunts the book as Nathaniel Emmons himself haunted the Beecher family. Immediately before Stern, who is actually Emmons, is introduced, there is a reference to "the deepest tragedy" in "our own family," which cannot be understood without reference to a peculiar society conditioned by a peculiar theology. Apparently this refers to the disastrous flight of Miss Rossiter's sister Emily, which results in her moral downfall. This flight was associated with Emily's reaction to Stern's sermons. Since, however, the episode does not actually occur in the narrator's family, it seems possible that Mrs. Stowe may here be referring—perhaps by a slip—to the greatest disaster in her own family, the loss of Fisher and Catharine's reaction to it. This also, it will be remembered, was made especially poignant by Emmons' preaching.

Throughout the book, Mrs. Stowe's references to Stern are undoubtedly sharpened by her own recollections of Emmons and her family's association with him. Her major account of his life, in Chapter 29, is, however, drawn from Professor Park's biography of Emmons, first published in 1861. It is a measure of the balance achieved by Mrs. Stowe that she is able to treat Stern with such detached and sympathetic irony. Robust people like "Grandmother Badger" are able to live with arch-Calvinist doctrines and retain their humanity, but for the sensitive, preaching like Stern's has a devastating effect. Nonetheless, and despite her own and her sister's sufferings at his hands, Mrs. Stowe pays tribute to Stern's courage and consistency: "In all this if there is something terrible and painful, there is something also which is grand, and in which we can take pride, as the fruit of our human nature. Peace to his ashes: he has learned better things ere now." To reach this point, Mrs. Stowe had traveled a long and painful journey.

The Boston Episcopalian establishment the children visit is partly modeled on "Nutplains," Harriet Beecher's mother's house. At "Nutplains," where some of Harriet Beecher's happiest childhood memories were centered, there was both a kind grandmother who was a defender of King George, and a strong-minded aunt who insisted that visiting children learn *both* catechisms, their father's and hers, and conceded that dissenting clergyman could be saved by God's "uncovenanted mercies" outside the Church. "Nutplains" undergoes a magic upgrading in the novel into a more than Bostonian mansion; in her own reminiscences Mrs. Stowe refers to it affectionately as "a lonely little farmhouse under the hill."[64]

Cloudland, where the children go to school, is Litchfield, with its beautiful hill country, its unusually cultivated society (mainly brought there by the famous law school), and its Academy.[65] The school in the book is a somewhat rose-colored version of the real one, but many of its actual graduates fervently praised Litchfield Female Academy. It had been founded in 1750 by Miss Sarah Pierce, with the purpose of teaching young ladies not only embroidery and music but such branches as Latin, sacred and profane history, and geography, which were usually considered essential only for young gentlemen. The school was not, as Mrs. Stowe implies, representative of New England academies, nor was it on principle coeducational, though some boys (including some male Beechers) were admitted. Most of its educational innovation was the work of Miss Pierce's nephew, John Pierce Brace, who is the original of Jonathan Rossiter. Under his regime the Litchfield Female Academy did indeed display some of the social liberalism and some of the academic seriousness attributed to it in the novel. There were, for instance, dancing parties which were open to the young gentlemen from the law school, and plays with Biblical subjects, including the one about Jephthah's daughter described in the novel. On the other hand pupils had to memorize a long and strict set of rules, accurately quoted in the novel, and Miss

Pierce sometimes threatened the unruly with the penalties of the next world as well as this. As in the novel, ambitious themes were assigned for discussion and writing. Harriet Beecher herself, at twelve, wrote a logical, highly conventional essay answering in the negative the question debated in the novel by Harry and Esther: "Can the Immortality of the Soul Be Proved by the Light of Nature?"[66]

Religious instruction in the Academy was attended to by Lyman Beecher, as it is in the novel by his prototype Dr. Avery. The Beecher theological position, stretching Calvinism to provide hope for nearly everybody, is described accurately enough in the novel, as are Beecher's methods of argument. The "Minister's wood-spell" comes from the *Autobiography*, as does the consociation meeting, with liquor and argument flowing freely (in the *Autobiography*, Beecher remembers this as a background for the prohibitionist movement that swept the clergy soon after).[67] Esther, Dr. Avery's intellectual daughter, is somehow unable to yield to the religious pressures even of such an admirable father, and refuses to be converted until she falls in love. Obviously she is an idealized combination of Catharine (whose middle name was Esther) and Harriet herself.

A number of characters and incidents are warmed over from previous use. The repetition of long passages from Mrs. Stowe's 1858 essay on "New England Ministers" has already been mentioned. *Uncle Tom's Cabin* provides the quite irrelevant "Raid on Oldtown" in Chapter 28, and is echoed less precisely by the children's flight from Old Crab Smith. In *The Pearl of Orr's Island*, Mrs. Stowe had already made use of a mysterious but unmistakably aristocratic child, who like Harry and Tina is adopted by a New England town when the mother dies. *The Minister's Wooing* provided still more material for *Oldtown Folks,* including one of its major characters, the satanic, brilliant grandson of Jonathan Edwards who in the later book is called Ellery Davenport but in *The Minister's Wooing* is identified as Edwards' actual grandson, Aaron Burr.

It is clear that Mrs. Stowe intended this book, for which she ransacked so ruthlessly her own and her husband's memories and her own earlier works, to be a masterpiece. It is less than that, and in some ways it is more interesting than if it were written with the control that masterpieces demand. It is most obviously interesting to students of American mores and religion. As Lowell told her, Mrs. Stowe could use her eyes, and she could, much of the time, use her imagination. Frequently she shows a talent for the evocative detail. One does not forget the dog's paws ticking up and down the meetinghouse aisle; or the turkey, languid from the cold, his wattles turned blue, lying over Caesar's shoulder while he is taken to the house so that grandmother can force down his throat Indian-meal mixed with peppercorns. A rather richer mixture of imagination with memory produces all Mrs. Stowe's best characters—all unfortunately minor characters and most, as the *Nation* observed, women. Lavishly, she gives her readers not one New England old maid but five: Miss Asphyxia, Aunt Lois, Miss Rossiter, the maid Polly, and the Anglican Miss Deborah. Each is different from the rest, and each is far more than a caricature out of stock. Sam Lawson, so much admired by nineteenth-century readers, is also more than a stock rendition of a cracker-barrel philosopher, though he is given too much of the story to carry, and at times breaks down under the burden.

Mrs. Stowe's imaginative perception extends from individuals to society. Her systematic review of the village social structure, illustrated in the church's seating arrangements, beginning neatly with the minister and leading families and trailing off into the Indian fringe, is a tour de force. Her explanation of the kind of preeminence which old families like the Rossiters enjoy, despite Oldtown's quite real social democracy, is more acute than a good deal of New England social research.

Above all, Mrs. Stowe uses her imagination effectively in dealing with history. In seeing Edwardsian Calvinism as an aberration from the New England tradition of bargaining with God, an aberration both triumphant and disastrous, Mrs. Stowe long anticipates the findings of historians. To do so took an enviable combination of firsthand knowledge and long-range vision. The opening image of New England's live coals, burning in isolation and obscurity beneath the surface, is the kind of image that is more than useful; it is illuminating.

Mrs. Stowe, moreover, has a point to make about intellectual history in general that is well worth the attention of historians. Ideas, she points out, though they do indeed dominate communities and nobody is immune from their influence, affect different people in different ways; as she puts it, "temperament gradually, but with irresistible power," modifies creed. As for the origins of "temperament," Mrs. Stowe knows well that individuality is partly a product of social forces, but of forces too complex to weigh and measure with confidence: "The humblest human being is the sum total of a column of figures which go back through centuries before he was born. Old Crab Smith and Miss Asphyxia, if their biographies were rightly written, would be found to be the result and out-come of certain moral and social forces, justly to discriminate which might puzzle a philosopher." This balance between determinism and freedom, one which many recent historians might well envy, is of course derived from Mrs. Stowe's theological inheritance. She does far more than simply to proclaim the necessity and fruitfulness of such a balanced vision; she triumphantly illustrates it again and again.

There is no question that *Oldtown Folks* is a valuable, and at times a masterly, piece of social and intellectual history. The question remains whether it is a good novel, or even a novel at all. Certainly Mrs. Stowe lacked some of the kinds of talent a novelist needs. She was never, for one thing, much interested in plot; except in *Uncle Tom's Cabin* (and there the success is partial) her plots are a failure; her dramatic structure is not only uninteresting, but even gets in the way of what she wants to say. In *Oldtown Folks* the plot has little to do with her announced purpose of recapturing ante-railroad New England and even, finally, takes her clear out of her chosen locale. The book is best where it is static, as in the first seven chapters, largely descriptive of Old-town. In the next section, chapters 8 through 15, the children find a new home and the major characters are in motion. This part is saved from dullness only by minor characters like Miss Asphyxia. In the next and longest section, in which everybody settles down again in Oldtown, the superb observation of village life generally makes the adventures of the children tolerable, and is interrupted only by the unconvincing excursion into Boston high life. In chapters 32 to 39 the book's pace again slows down while Cloudland, its school and its minister, are described almost as successfully as Oldtown. Then, in the last chapters, the pace of events quickens and the book runs rapidly downhill. By this time, all Mrs. Stowe wanted was to mail the last chapters. Since she has no more to say, she relies on coincidence and melodrama, heavily coated with sentimentality and liberally spiced with high life. Harry turns out to be a missing heir and even Tina preaches—and she preaches moreover the simplest of moralities with no undergirding of theology. Inevitably, when the Oldtown people come to Boston for the wedding and are forced again to go through their paces, now in the presence of the quality, they become quaint.

Mrs. Stowe's style cannot very profitably be discussed in terms of conventional literary influences. Like everybody who writes, she was influenced by what she had read. Like everybody who read at all and was brought up when she was, she was influenced by Scott—in her case not the Scott of *Ivanhoe,* whose influence in America Mark Twain and others deplore, but the Scott of *The Heart of Mid-Lothian,* the Scott who turned to native subjects and the lives of the humble, the Scott for whom Lyman Beecher raised his ban on fiction. She read Maria Edgeworth early, as a young woman learned to like Madame de Staël's *Corinne,* and never got over the Byron craze that swept New England in her youth.

Mrs. Stowe, as some of her biographers point out, was not much interested in literature. She was a prolific professional author, but much of her production, in tracts and magazine pieces, can be called subliterary. Despite her friendship with Holmes and her warm relations with the Fields, she took almost no part in New England literary life. In the heyday of the Genteel Tradition, when veneration for the past and conscious imitation of approved models were all too common, it was not really a disadvantage to live outside literary circles.

Most of the time Mrs. Stowe frankly refused to bother about style at all, except for a few specific purposes. She insisted that her best work came from God. In his own way, even so skeptical a critic as Edmund Wilson accepts this statement: her best writing came from her subconscious.

In *Oldtown Folks,* she uses at least three styles. One, the one in which she labors her way through the plot, is the standard polite diction of her day. She is more informal than most of her contemporaries. Setpieces of elaborate description are rare, and mock-heroic diction, that favorite device of Victorian authors dealing with the humble, is employed only rarely, when she is tired of her material.

The style Mrs. Stowe worked at hardest, and one in which she was a pioneer, is dialect. Sam Lawson at his best, Miss Nervy teaching Latin, and Grandmother needling Aunt Lois speak with originality and point. Their utterance is not at all in the already conventional vein of the comic Yankee, because Mrs. Stowe's purpose is not patronizing or trivial. It is significant that some of her sharpest theological criticism is delivered through characters who speak dialect. Miss Asphyxia, accused by Grandmother of having a hard heart, tellingly asks what else she *could* have, not being elected, but makes it clear that she considers herself quite as good for all worldly purposes as any church member. Sam Lawson puts the perennial question graphically: "Ef a man's cut off his hands, it ain't right to require him to chop wood. Wal, Polly, she says he'd no business to cut his hands off; and so he ought to be required to chop the wood all the same. Wal, I told her it was Adam chopped our hands off."

In dealing with rural New England speech, Mrs. Stowe made an exception to her usual carelessness about detail. Writing Fields, just as she was finishing *Oldtown Folks* and while batches of proof were coming in, she complained about the proofreader she usually trusted:

There is one thing I wish to have you expound to my accurate friend and family connection Mr. Bigelow, when

he sends my proof of yankee talk. The genuine yankee
always calls things this ere and that are.

> This ere woman and that are man.

Now I always spell them according to the sound this *ere*
and that *are*—but my accurate friend Mr. Bigelow always
alters it & wont let me print 'that *are*' simply because being
a contraction of *there* it is more accurate to spell 'that 'ere'.
Now please ask him to have a printed *my* way in future."[68]

The third style Mrs. Stowe uses, and the one that
comes most clearly from her subconscious, is the prophetic. If we cannot accept her own view of her inspi-
ration, we can perhaps admit that she was a prophet at
third hand. As she says, the taste of all New Englanders
was formed on the King James Bible, and in her case
the Bible was mediated through a tradition of lively evangelical preaching. In *Oldtown Folks* Mrs. Stowe puts on
the prophetic mantle only briefly and rarely, and when
she does it fits; she is talking about her Israel and its
decline.

In terms of American literary history, Mrs. Stowe's
New England novels are a part of the beginning of the
local color movement.[69] She could draw, it is true, on a
considerable number of minor genre pieces, a large rep-
ertory of Yankee dialect humor, and an oral tradition
of folklore. She did make use of all these. Mrs. Lydia
Sigourney, for one—an author known to Mrs. Stowe—
made some attempt to treat religious history in dialect.
A comic farmer, in her *Sketch of Connecticut,* criticizes the
ways of Episcopalians and Methodists.[70] But Mrs. Sigourney's treatment, both of Connecticut and its religion,
is from outside. She plays the role of an aristocratic visitor, who finds rustic ways morally admirable but styl-
istically amusing.

Mrs. Stowe usually avoids this tone, and is among the

first writers to render the scene and speech of an American region with respect as well as fidelity. *Oldtown Folks* barely antedates the principal works of Bret Harte, who does not attain this standard, and of Edward Eggleston, who does. All the New England local writers who followed Mrs. Stowe were, like her, motivated by nostalgia for what was passing, but most were much more sentimental than their predecessor. Until *Poganuc People,* Mrs. Stowe does not use the sturdy New England virtues, as many others did, to attack the faults of newcomers.

Judged solely as a specimen of regional literature, *Sam Lawson's Oldtown Fireside Stories,* in which Mrs. Stowe used up her surplus *Oldtown* material, may contain her best work.[71] The dialect is meticulous, the folklore and legend rich, the touch fairly light. *Fireside Stories* gives us an idea of what *Oldtown Folks* might have amounted to, if Mrs. Stowe had been trying to portray the surface of a time and a place, and trying nothing more.

If we see *Oldtown Folks* in relation to the regional movement, it achieves an honorable place. To compare it to the greatest works of American fiction is equally illuminating, but the result is less flattering. Hawthorne, Melville, and Mark Twain have all been occasionally invoked in the course of the recent revival of interest in Mrs. Stowe. It is true that both *Moby Dick* and the *Scarlet Letter* deal with the same problem as *Oldtown Folks,* the evil in the universe and man's perception of it through the medium of Christian theology. But there the resemblance stops. Melville and Hawthorone were able to organize a novel to make their philosophical and theological points; Mrs. Stowe had to make her points either through minor characters or in her own person; her narrative has little to do with them.

Neither Melville nor Hawthorne, though both nodded, could ever have written the most conventional and sentimental parts of *Oldtown Folks*. Mark Twain, the most uneven of major writers, could, and the comparison of Mrs. Stowe with her Hartford neighbor has something to tell us. *Huckleberry Finn,* like most of *Oldtown Folks,* was written in the prosperous section of Hartford known as Nook Farm, a place of mansions, ample grounds, liberal Beecherized religion, and other evidences of Victorian culture.[72] Like Mrs. Stowe, Clemens looked back from this Hartford to the time and place of his childhood, and sometimes he looked with regret for what had gone. Like her, he alternated between a lofty and a colloquial style.[73] At her best she used regional speech almost as effectively as he did, and she did it first.

There is, however, one big difference between the two Hartford neighbors in addition to the obvious one in creative capacity. This is in their attitude toward the American past. Mark Twain, harking back to the time and place of his youth, praised it even less wholeheartedly than Mrs. Stowe. Like her, he subscribed fully to the official American goals of liberty and democracy. Again like Mrs. Stowe, Clemens loved and sometimes exaggerated the uncomplicated kind of freedom and equality which seemed in retrospect characteristic of a preindustrial society. But Clemens, like most major American writers, was in some moods far more skeptical than Mrs. Stowe about the degree to which prewar America—or perhaps any society—had ever achieved real freedom or equality.

No doubt Clemens' greater alienation is explainable partly in regional terms, and partly in the far more complicated terms of individual development. There is, however, at least one clear source for this difference. Clemens probably felt somewhat ambivalent about the secular half of American tradition. About the religious half he felt no ambivalence at all: Protestant orthodoxy he obsessively hated. Mrs. Stowe, despite her sufferings and her doubts, found New England Calvinism more than half admirable, and its view of the world more than half true.

Clemens' more alienated stance was not always to his advantage as a writer. He could not deal as convincingly as Mrs. Stowe with some kinds of people. Aunt Polly is a conventional figure and not much more; she is not nearly as interesting as Mrs. Stowe's old maids. But Huck, who has seceded from society, sees it more clearly than does Sam Lawson, who does not secede but hangs around on the fringes. Huck cannot be tolerated by solid citizens, and cannot be patronized; Sam is tolerated and patronized, occasionally even by his author. Thus Huck's outside vision can serve as the main instrument for Mark Twain's comments on society and its official beliefs. Mrs. Stowe has much to say about these matters, and much of it is shrewd and original, but she cannot say it through any of her characters. The main figures of her story are trivial constructs, and the minor characters, who are often believable and interesting, are part of her social picture and cannot look straight at it. Thus she has to interrupt herself, forget her story, and comment on New England in her own person—as historian or prophet but not as novelist.

Oldtown Folks is not a great novel or a great work of art; it may not be a novel at all. Whatever it be called—a series of sketches, a historical essay with interpolated plot—it is an uneven performance. With all its faults it is an interesting and important book. In it a woman of keen intelligence and sharp perception has drawn on a lifetime of outward observation and inner experience. As a New England writer should, and as few writers of any kind manage to do successfully, Mrs. Stowe gives us a look beneath the surface of a society: at the live coals glowing.

5

Jonathan Edwards
and America

*In 1984, I was surprised to be invited to present a keynote
speech for a conference on Jonathan Edwards to be held at
Wheaton College, an institution with an explicit evangelical
commitment. This turned out to be one of the most successful
conferences I have ever attended. The reason was simple: that
everyone there, speakers and invited guests, was in some way
fascinated by the great theologian. Some participants had a
deep personal devotion to Edwardsian theology. One young
man I met had gone so far as to name his daughter Jerusha,
after Edwards's daughter. On the other hand, many were
scholars with entirely secular viewpoints, and were part of
the extraordinary recent flowering of Edwards scholarship.
Some of these were fresh from the great deposit of Edwards
papers at Yale, much of it still unpublished. What was needed for an opening talk was something like an invocation. I
tried to write one that would be appropriate for the various
kinds of participants, and for the place. The proceedings of
the conference, including this essay, were published in 1988
by Oxford University Press as* Jonathan Edwards and
the American Experience, *ed. Nathan O. Hatch and
Harry S. Stout.*

I have a friend who is nothing if not frank. When I told him that I had been asked to give a keynote speech for a conference on Jonathan Edwards he said, "Now Henry, why you? You don't know all that much about Edwards." He was of course quite right, I don't, and I realized this rather acutely when I saw the list of formidable Edwards experts who were going to assemble here. Then I thought, maybe that is *why* I am asked to do this. A keynote speech—a term taken over from American politics—is not expected to be a profound scholarly inquiry. What is it supposed to do? It is supposed to help create an atmosphere of enthusiasm and unity, and perhaps to gloss over deep differences of opinion. Maybe this cannot be done by people profoundly involved in passionate argument, and can best be attempted by somebody distinctly on the periphery.

Aside from not knowing too much, I have one other qualification for this job. I have long found Edwards deeply interesting, sometimes repellent, often attractive and moving. And we all know the importance, in relation to real understanding, of lively affections. When I first read as a graduate student, that true virtue consists in the disinterested love of being in general, my immediate response was not "how clever, how well-put" but rather "how right, how beautiful." Long years later, after teaching a semester run-through of the history of American religion, I once offered to teach an undergraduate seminar on any topic we had covered. I prepared myself to deal with the churches and Vietnam, or the churches and civil rights. Instead, I got the most requests for a seminar on Edwards. Not very many requests of course—there were eight students. All had their special attitudes toward Edwards. At least three were part of the new-evangelical movement that was flowering on the campuses in the wake of the political movements of the sixties. (Incidentally, these were disappointed as they got to know Edwards better—he was not what they wanted him to be.) Of the others one, the best, had a Catholic education, which meant—at that time—a solid grounding in philosophy and theology. At least one was an intelligent and articulate skeptic. We read most of the Edwards writing that was then generally accessible, and a lot of Edwards criticism from Oliver Wendell Holmes and Leslie Stephen through Parrington to—you guessed it—Perry Miller. We arrived at no consensus, and I think this was perhaps the course that I most enjoyed teaching at Berkeley.

More interesting than the question, "Why me?" is the question "Why you?" Why is it that Edwards has attracted not just a passing glance, but the devotion of years of hard work on the part of so many fine scholars? Is it because you believe him, love him, admire him? Is it because you find him complex and baffling, a perfectly engaging puzzle, a figure eternally subject to profound reinterpretation? Is it because he seems to some of you, as he did to Miller and others, to offer a key to the understanding of American culture? I suspect that all these and other powerful attractions helped to incline your wills in the direction of attending this conference.

It is an intriguing fact that, according to M.X. Lesser's massive Edwards bibliography, the number of dissertations on Edwards has doubled in each decade since 1940.[1] And I think I can say, since I am something of an outsider to this field, that recently the quality has gone up as well as the volume. Yet, as with most interesting subjects, the more we know about Edwards, the harder he becomes to deal with. We have learned for instance that he did *not* develop on the far frontier isolated from European thought, that he was *not* suddenly turned on in college by reading Locke, indeed that he was not really a Lockeian. If you hear a noise, it is the crackling of burning lecture notes.

Who and what was Edwards *really*? It is impossible to answer that question without the divine and spiritual light to which I claim no access. Since I am trained as a historian all I can do is try to suggest, in most of the rest of this talk, what Edwards has meant to some kinds of Americans during the two centuries leading up to the present explosion of Edwards scholarship. I want to try to deal with motivation as well as understanding, to discuss the power of attraction and repulsion exerted by Edwards on several kinds of people in several historical periods. But before I do this I want to make it clear that I am not intending to patronize the past. Much as I admire the Edwards scholarship of today, I do not want to imply that in the past people saw Edwards through a mist of prejudice, and now we look at him in the clear light of objectivity. I assume that we all look at Edwards from where we are, and that this will always be so.

Most of us, in our first courses in historiography, heard a lot about the dangers of presentism. I agree that it is a disastrous mistake to push and hack one's subject matter so that it will fit into fashionable categories. This is clearly bad, and Edwards has suffered from it. But another kind of presentism gives most of its vitality to historical study, the kind that after rigorous discipline and close study of the sources asks the questions that arise from the most important concerns of the present. I think that the best Edwards scholarship has always done this. From each of the successive views of Edwards that I want briefly to present there is much to learn, about the preoccupations and assumptions of successive periods in intellectual history, but also about Edwards himself.

The first Edwards, of course, was that of course, was

that of his disciples. According to Samuel Hopkins, perhaps his most devoted follower:

> President Edwards, in the esteem of all the judicious, who
> were well-acquainted with him, either personally, or by his
> writings, was one of the *greatest best* and *most useful* of
> men, that have lived in this age.... And that this distin-
> guished light has not shone in vain, there are a cloud of
> witnesses.... And there is reason to hope, that though now
> he is dead, he will yet speak for a great while yet to come,
> to the great comfort and advantage of the church of Christ;
> that his publications will produce a yet greater harvest, as
> an addition to his joy and crown of rejoicing in the day of
> the Lord.[2]

How many ardent young men followed Edwards as
closely as they could is a question much debated among
recent scholars.[3] It seems clear that there were several
hundred of these all-out Edwardsians, most of them intelligent, articulate, and poor. By the 1820s or '30s the
New Divinity, developed directly from Edwards' theology, was being forced into rural strongholds in New
England, where it long survived. Yet even in the centers
of moderate Calvinism, where Edwards' teachings were
more and more modified to fit nineteenth-century optimism, Edwards was yet venerated by Congregationalist
and Presbyterian divines. Timothy Dwight, one of the
first of the long list of modifiers, called Edwards "That
moral Newton, and that second Paul."[4] Lyman Beecher,
the most powerful spokesman of nineteenth-century
neo-Calvinism, made in his youth a statement he was
never to retract: "I had read Edwards' Sermons. There's
nothing comes within a thousand miles of them now."[5]
In a statement made by Edwards Amasa Park in 1839,
one can hear the dying gasp of Edwardsian loyalty, struggling with the Genteel Tradition and losing:

We bow before this father of our New England theology
with the profoundest veneration. We read his precious volumes with awe in tears. We are so superstitious, that we
almost fear to be called profane for lisping a word against
the perfect balancing of his character. And yet we can not
help wishing that he had been somewhat more of a brother
and somewhat less of a champion. . . . We need and crave a
theology, as sacred and spiritual as his, and moreover one
that we can take with us into the flower-garden, and to the
top of some goodly hill, and in a sail over a tasteful lake,
and into the saloons of music, and to the galleries of the
painter and the sculptor, and to the repasts of social joy,
and to all those humanizing scenes where virtue holds her
sway not merely as that generic and abstract duty of a "love
to being in general," but also as the more familiar grace of
a love to some beings in particular.[6]

Long before this, while the New Divinity was gaining
its triumphs, even while Edwards was still alive, he was
being rejected in several different ways by the protag-
onists of the Enlightenment. In New England from
Charles Chauncy on, many took on the formidable task
of refuting his arguments, and of showing that these
were not only mistaken but immoral. The doctrine of
necessity was crippling to the conscience. The idea of
double predestination was an insult to the moral and
benevolent God who established the law of nature
and gave us the ability to know and follow it. To Stiles
and Witherspoon, practical men like most college presidents, the New Divinity was fanatical and obscurantist.
To those who moved beyond liberal Christianity toward
Enlightened skepticism Edwards' whole subject matter
was without interest. Nobody expressed this better than
John Adams:

Mr. Adams leaves to Homer and Virgil, to Tacitus and
Quintilian, to Mahomet and Calvin, to Edwards and Priest-

ley, or, if you will, to Milton's angels reasoning high in pandemonium, all their acute speculations about fate, destiny, foreknowledge absolute, necessity, and predestination. He thinks it problematical whether there is, or ever will be, more than one Being capable of understanding this vast subject.[7]

Quite different in spirit from this sort of eighteenth-century dismissal was the nineteenth-century revulsion against Edwards as a cruel monster, dangerous because of his great talents. Oliver Wendell Holmes expressed it well:

It is impossible that people of ordinary sensibilities should have listened to his torturing discourses without becoming at last sick of hearing of infinite horrors and endless agonies.

Of Edwards' uncompromising insistence on the total depravity of unregenerate children Holmes asks:

It is possible that Edwards read the text mothers love so well, Suffer little *vipers* to come unto me, and forbid them not, for of such is the kingdom of God.[8]

Harriet Beecher Stowe described the effect of Edwardsian doctrines like this:

It is a fact that the true tragedy of New England life, its deep, unutterable pathos, its endurances and its sufferings, all depended upon, and were woven into, this constant wrestling of thought with infinite problems which could not be avoided, and which saddened the day of almost every one who grew up under it....

Thus was this system calculated, like a skilful engine of torture, to produce all the mental anguish of the most perfect sense of helplessness with the most torturing sense of responsibility.[9]

Mrs. Stowe's Hartford neighbor Samuel Clemens carried this revulsion much further. After reading the *Freedom of the Will,* Clemens wrote his minister:

> ... continuously until near midnight I wallowed and reeked with Jonathan in his insane debauch; rose immediately refreshed and fine at 10 this morning, but with a strange and haunting sense of having been on a three days' tear with a drunken lunatic. ... All through the book is the glare of a resplendent intellect gone mad—a marvellous spectacle. No, not *all* through the book—the drunk does not come on till the last third, where what I take to be Calvinism and its God begins to show up and shine red and hideous in the glow from the fires of hell, their only right and proper adornment. By God I was ashamed to be in such company.[10]

It is not difficult to sympathize with these outraged Victorians. I agree with Holmes. To modify his statement slightly, if we can read the imprecatory sermons without horror it is because of a failure of imagination. Consistent Calvinism is admired in recent times chiefly by people to whom it has never occurred that its doctrines might really describe the true state of affairs. If one is seriously to follow Edwards, recent scholarship has made clear, one must accept his doctrine of Hell not as a minor blemish on his intellectual system, but as essential to it.[11] One must accept as true his masterly descriptions of intolerable and interminable suffering. Still more difficult, to be a real Edwardsian one must come to terms with his insistence that God hates sinners and holds them in the utmost contempt. Once a human being has had his chance, and has not been able to accept it, God will never feel the slightest pity for him. If a person is saved, part of his duty will be to love all aspects of God forever, including his vindictive justice. Thus he will have to learn to rejoice in the rightness and beauty of eternal suffering for others. To be a real follower of Edwards, one must moreover come to terms with little Phoebe Bartlett, four years old, sure of her own salvation, sorry for her sisters, predicting their death, weeping over the sin of stealing plums but blaming her sister for talking her into it, and expressing plummy love for her minister, Mr. Edwards.

For many nineteenth-century Americans, especially in New England, it was not possible to pick and choose. They had been brought up to believe that Edwards' doctrines or something like them were saving truth. After this, to reject them meant a major emotional struggle, which left its marks. The life of Mrs. Stowe's family had been tragically affected by the preaching of a major Edwardsian. Holmes, writing to Mrs. Stowe about Calvinism, describes his upbringing in an image of almost Edwardsian power:

> I have found myself like a nursery-tree, growing up with labels of this and that article of faith wired to my limbs. The labels have dropped off, but the wires are only buried in my flesh, which has grown over them.... I do not believe you or I can ever get the iron of Calvinism out of our souls.[12]

Clemens, not being a New Englander, had not had quite this sort of exposure to intellectual Calvinism. Yet many of works, and still more clearly his marginal comments and letters, bear witness to his prolonged early exposure to the grim aspects of evangelical Protestantism, his fervent revulsion against it, and the fact that its ghost continued to haunt him. These Victorians who hated

Calvinism took it and Edwards seriously, and we should take seriously their anguished rejection.

In the early twentieth century, instead of rebelling against Edwards, it became possible to patronize him. Countless writers portrayed him as a talented but tragic figure, who could have been a great poet, a great philosopher, or a great scientist if he hadn't got mired in outworn theology. V. L. Parrington's account, more balanced than one might expect, contains several pages of eloquent appreciation but ends in lament:

> The intellectual powers were his, but the inspiration was lacking; like Cotton Mather before him, he was the unconscious victim of a decadent ideal and a petty environment. Cut off from fruitful intercourse with other thinkers, drawn away from the stimulating field of philosophy into the arid realm of theology, it was his fate to devote his noble gifts to the thankless task of re-imprisoning the mind of New England within a system from which his nature and his powers summoned him to unshackle it. He was called to be a transcendental emancipator, but he remained a Calvinist.[13]

Rather similarly, Henry Bamford Parkes lamented in 1930 that Edwards had abandoned his promising early pantheism for Calvinism.

> To have experienced those realities of human nature which are the foundation of Christianity, and yet to reject Calvinism, would have required, in a Connecticut schoolboy, in 1721, a wisdom almost superhuman; but because Edwards lacked that wisdom, his career is, in its hidden implications, the most tragic in American history....
>
> The dark stream of Calvinism is but a tributary to the flood of American culture; Edwards merely carried to its extreme a tendency brought from Europe; in spite of his patriotism he was not really an American.[14]

It is harder for us to admire the progressive patron-
izers than to respect the forthright rejecters of Victorian
times. Patronizing Edwards, they remind us of Edwards'
own description of his own liberal contemporaries patronizing the great reformers of the sixteenth century:

> Indeed most of these new writers, at the same time that
> they have represented the doctrines of these ancient and
> eminent divines as in the highest degree ridiculous, and
> contrary to common sense, in an ostentation of a very gen-
> erous charity, have allowed that they were honest, well-
> meaning men; yea, it may be, some of them, as though it
> were in great condescension and compassion for them, have
> allowed that they did pretty well for the day in which they
> lived . . . living in the gloomy caves of superstition [they]
> fondly embraced, and demurely and zealously taught the
> most absurd, silly, and monstrous opinions, worthy of the
> greatest contempt of gentlemen possessed of that noble and
> generous freedom of thought, which happily prevail in this
> age of light and inquiry.[15]

This remains a sufficient put down of liberal presentism. Yet I think one should remember how hard it was
in the early twentieth century to approve any ideas that
seemed to reject democratic progress. In a sense Parkes
was right: there was no place for Edwards in the rise of
American civilization. More recently Norman Fiering
has warned us in a truly eloquent passage that Edwards
was almost alone in the eighteenth century in rejecting
the idea of the universal moral sense and the essential
goodness of the common man. If we follow him in this
we must realize that we are rejecting the most valuable
heritage of the Enlightenment:

> Only the two great wars of the twentieth century and the
> Holocaust have been able to shake into ruins, at least tem-

porarily, the psychological optimism of the Shaftesbury-Hutcheson gospel of the innate goodness of man.[16]

It is out of the era of war and holocaust that the most powerful and interesting recent interpretation of Edwards has come: Edwards as a modern or post-modern intellectual. In 1949, Perry Miller presented him as one of the long and honorable line of American intellectuals who indicted utilitarian liberalism, complacency, and the profit motive, in a word (not Miller's) Babbittry. Edwards attacked the Philistines, moreover, not in the name of transcendence but in behalf of "what seems rather a glorified naturalism."[17]

Miller has been well and thoroughly jumped on, by consistent naturalists, consistent theologians, and worst of all, by historians who convict him of either misreading or not reading some of the evidence. It is quite clear that Edwards was not any kind of naturalist.

Yet I think something is left of Edwards' modernity (asserted by others besides Miller) if only in terms of analogy. Edwards certainly was an enemy of complacency, and so are most important American writers, including of course Perry Miller. He is one of a long succession of American Jeremiahs, brooding over the grievious faults of their strange Israel. And there is something in Edwards' doctrine of moral necessity highly compatible with much modern thought. We are prevented from doing what we should do, even what we want to do, by our upbringing, our culture, our psychological formation—in short, our diseased will. It is understandable that Miller's *Edwards*, for all its many mistakes, sparked the revival of Edwards scholarship. It remains an interesting book, primarily because it was written by an interesting man.

In 1966, Alan Heimert, who might possibly be described as Miller's Samuel Hopkins, published his *Religion and the American Mind*.[18] With much learning and many exaggerations, Heimert associated Edwards and his followers with the American radical tradition from the Revolution on. One might say that where Miller had made Edwards an intellectual of the 1920s, his younger disciple made Edwards an intellectual of the 1930s. Heimert's book, partly because of a few unfortunate statements, called forth an extraordinary barrage of heavy artillery. And yet I don't think that Heimert was blown clear out of the water.

Edwards himself was not a social radical, not indeed directly interested in issues of social welfare, though Hopkins reports he was personally charitable to the poor. He was no precursor of Jeffersonian, still less of Jacksonian democracy. He had nothing in common with the generally populist content of later American radicalism. He was in fact one of the greatest opponents of the theory that what is popular is right.

Yet it remains quite true that he offered no comfort to the wealthy and well-placed in their complacency, and that his closest followers were overwhelmingly among the radical supporters of the American Revolution. Heimert, even more clearly than other historians, shows us the reasons for this, the association of virtue, frugality, and sound doctrine with America—of decadence, luxury, and lukewarm religion with England.

There is even a useful analogy between the attraction of the New Divinity in the late eighteenth century and that of Marxism in the 1930s. Both attracted the young, the poor, and the intelligent. Both demanded total surrender and therefore appealed to those who wanted to give themselves completely to a cause. Both asserted that there was only one good force in the world, that from this only came all legitimacy, and that half-measures were evil. Survivors of the thirties find something familiar in the curse of Meroz invoked effectively against liberals.

One more major view of Edwards, related to that of Perry Miller but yet quite different, arose out of the successive revivals of religion in America, beginning with the neo-orthodox movement of the '30s, '40s, and '50s. Miller himself was friendly to this movement but outside it; he and others like him have been called "atheists for Niebuhr." The *theists* for Niebuhr saw a different Edwards, not a precursor of modern existentialism but a serious theologian in the tradition of Augustine and Calvin. It should be noted that Reinhold Niebuhr himself made very little use of Edwards and at one point disapproved his absolutist ethic as crippling to social responsibility.[19] His brother H. Richard Niebuhr, more interested than Reinhold in the study of the American religious past, listed Edwards' *Nature of True Virtue* along with books by Pascal, Barth, Calvin and others among those books that had most influenced his own philosophy of life.[20]

As early as 1932, Joseph Haroutunian treated the history of New England theology as a long, tragic decline from Edwards' profundity, and announced in his preface that today's world could, *in its own way*, appreciate Calvinism better than the recent past.

Whereas the language of Calvinism is in disrepute, the elements of good sense in Calvinism must always remain wherever there is good sense.... The optimism and the humanism of the nineteenth century have already lost their rational quality.

It is probable that a revival of the "tragic sense of life," together with the wisdom and sobriety which grow out of it, should be forthcoming. It is necessary that men rediscover the truths once signified by the doctrines of divine sovereignty and divine grace, of predestination and election, of depravity and regeneration...

If the humanitarianism of Channing is modern, a postmodern mind is already in the making. Its spirit is as yet skeptical and "naturalistic." It believes itself to be in an alien world. In order to become religious, it must become reconciled with God.[21]

By 1966, when Conrad Cherry wrote his analysis of the theology of Edwards, the neo-orthodox movement had come and gone, leaving an important residue, at least in the study of the American past. This residue is quite apparent in Cherry's introduction:

Whatever quarrel one may have with the specific features of the theologies of such thinkers as Karl Barth and Reinhold Niebuhr, they have, in diverse ways, reclaimed Augustinian and Calvinist categories in order to prick the contemporary conscience, wean man away from religious sentimentality, and throw him up against the hard reality of a God who judges as well as forgives...the once deplorable doctrine of predestination symbolizes man's precarious situation in the presence of a God whose will cannot be reduced to our purposes.[22]

Writing from this perspective Cherry totally rejects Miller's existentialist Edwards. Edwards did not reject either the Puritan past or covenant theology, he remained "first and last a Calvinist theologian," not neo-orthodox but essentially orthodox.

The mass revival of religion of the 1950s, often heartily disapproved of by neo-orthodox and other intellectuals, led to a reemphasis on Edwards as a critical revivalist. In 1959 John E. Smith, introducing Edwards' *Religious Affections* said that our present religious situation enables us to understand him as perhaps never before. For we are falling or have fallen into some of the very pitfalls he sought to avoid; we are in a better position than any age since Edwards to understand the profundity of his contribution to theological thinking . . .

He has given us a means of exposing the pseudo religions of moralism, sentimentality, and social conformity.

While legitimizing revival and "heart religion," Edwards, Smith points out

failed to fall in with revivalism at two crucial points: he denied that the urgency of believing provides any criterion for the truth of religion or the sincerity of the believer, and he was unwilling to follow the pattern of most revivalists and set the religious spirit over against learning and intellect. For Edwards the Word must come in truth as well as in power.[23]

In the current revival of evangelical Protestantism still another Edwards has been powerfully put before us, Edwards the serious and devoted student of the millennium. A long series of historians, clearly influenced by the new apocalyptic possibilities of the nuclear era, writing from both secular and religious points of view, have brought back to the surface a major part of Christian history long understated and explained away—the study of prophecy and the prediction of the last days. Starting with important hints from Richard Niebuhr, Edwards' millennial and apocalyptic thought has been thoroughly explored by a series of careful and insightful scholars including C.C. Goen and Stephen J. Stein.[24] Always eagerly searching the signs of the times for evidence of God's intentions, Edwards in his most optimistic moment in 1743 believed that he saw the millennium dawning in America.

In my opinion the Edwards that emerges from scholars affected by recent religious movements, the Edwards who is primarily Calvinist, revivalist, and millenarian, is closer to the truth than Edwards the modern existentialist, so daringly and unforgettably presented by Perry Miller. It is valuable to have Edwards seen once more as a major figure in American religious as well as intellectual history. Yet a word of caution is necessary. The best theological students of Edwards know well, but some semi-popular writers have forgotten that Edwards is not really ancestral to any of the major kinds of nineteenth- or twentieth-century American religion. His millennial predictions about America have nothing in common with the foolish chauvinism of many nineteenth-century preachers. Destiny, to Edwards, was never really Manifest. He clearly disapproved the humanist and liberal tendency that has issued in the nearly secular humanitarianism of the mainline churches today. Populistic and uncritical revivalists who have flourished in all periods surely cannot claim as their ally the author of *Religious Affections*. Fundamentalists can have little commerce with a man who never feared that the discoveries of contemporary science could be in contradiction to religious truth. Dispensationalists are a long way from a man who thought that the worst trials promised by revelation were over and that the new day might already have dawned. What are most churchgoers to do with a man who, according to the best recent analysis, "explicitly denied the efficacy of petitionary prayer to bring about external change in the world"?[25]

I have tried so far to suggest a few of the main interpretations of Edwards—there are of course many others—that have succeeded each other in the past. It is time to ask where we are left. After this keynote, can the convention agree on a platform? On a few planks, I think.

First, I think we can agree that Edwards was somehow a great man, whether we admire him most as artist, psychologist, preacher, theologian, or philosopher. Second, I think we can probably agree on what was the starting point and motive of all his work.

> To one cardinal principle Edwards was faithful—the conception of the majesty and sufficiency of God; and this polar idea provides the clue to both his philosophical and theological systems.[26]

This was said not by Haroutunian or Cherry, not by any of the editors of the Yale edition, not by Norman Fiering, but by Vernon Louis Parrington and it seems to me undeniable. Third, I think we can agree that Edwards like all thinkers much worth studying was fully of his own time and yet transcended it. He has had a great deal to say to people who loved and admired him, people who were horrified and haunted by him, people of many kinds of the eighteenth, nineteenth, and twentieth centuries. He seems both inexhaustible and impossible to pin down.

There are some other things on which I think we cannot and will not agree. First, is his work a massive, successful structure, or a majestic, instructive, and brilliant failure? There are many ways to ask this question. Can we understand the preacher who in one sermon tells his listeners to seek Christ: "You need not hesitate one moment, but may run to him and cast yourself upon him; you will certainly be graciously and meekly received by him,"[27] and in others makes it clear that nothing will

avail unless one has been totally changed by the uncontrollable power of the spirit? Probably there is no real
inconsistency of doctrine here but is there not an inconsistency in homiletic effect?

As for his theology, I am certainly not qualified to
criticize it, but hope some of the theologians here will
tell me whether there is or is not a contradiction between
believing, on the one hand, in a God that is both wholly
other and wholly transcendent, and on the other hand,
analyzing in detail his nature and intentions. Regarding
Edwards' philosophy Fiering, who regards him as a great
and profound thinker, leaves the question of validity
wide open:

> A difficult question, and one we need not debate here, is
> whether Edwards' primary, objective, ontological founda-
> tion for virtue is philosophically or even theologically
> tenable.

Regarding his effort to reconcile responsibility and predestination Fiering says

> It would be absurd to say that Edwards succeeded in dis-
> solving this theological mystery (all of his solutions seem to
> be sophistical) . . . [28]

Finally, I come to what is for me the most difficult
and interesting question of all. This is the question raised
by James Hoopes: "Many modern scholars," says
Hoopes, "have no idea what it feels like to perceive holiness [this seems to me a massive understatement], and
those who do can no more describe the sensation to the
rest of us than one can tell a man blind since birth what
it feels like to see."[29] To bring together the affections,
the understanding, and the will, Edwards has to rely on

the sixth spiritual sense, "a Spiritual and Divine Light, immediately imparted to the soul by God, of a different nature from any that is obtained by natural means."[30] This supreme and crucial faculty is necessarily, for unregenerate people, both indefinable and unverifiable. Perhaps Edwards' greatest achievements as a writer is that he comes close through his poetic powers to achieving the impossible. He almost manages to prove to the unilluminated the logical necessity of this supernatural illumination, and even to tell us what it is like.

This can be put in simpler terms, arising out of the history of Edwards studies and the makeup of this conference. Is it possible to have a fruitful discussion of a great religious thinker with the frank participation of believers, rejecters, and agnostics? This seems to me a question which a conference on this topic, in this place, needs to face head-on.

III The Enlightenment and After

6

The Constitution and the Enlightened Consensus

My Enlightenment in America *has occasionally been criticized for concentrating on religion rather than on politics. This was a deliberate choice, made in part because the political divisions, theories, and great accomplishments of late nineteenth-century Americans had been dealt with so much, their underlying attitudes toward human nature so little. I did not by any means want to ignore politics, but rather to cast some fresh light on that subject by looking first at religion, broadly defined. After all, eighteenth-century theorists nearly always treated moral philosophy first, political philosophy second.*

When I was asked to give the opening lecture in a series on the Constitution at Oregon State University in the bicentennial year 1987, I saw this as an opportunity to correct a little the balance of my work. However, after rereading the Constitutional debates and reading as much as I could in the immense and often illuminating recent discussion of them, I decided that the best hope of saying something fresh was once more to look at politics in terms of underlying assumptions. The Constitutional debates, read from this point of view, reveal beneath fierce disagreements a deep, taken-for-granted unity among Federalists and Antifederalists, conservatives and liberals, the party of commerce and the party of virtue—even between Calvinists and Deists. This underlying agreement, soon to disappear, seemed to me to have a lot to do with the astonishing success of 1787.

This essay is reprinted by permission of the Oregon State University Constitution Bicentennial Project Committee.

One of the most important facts about the Constitution is that it was written exactly two hundred years ago, in 1787. If it had been written even a few years earlier or later it would be a very different document. The Constitution was made during a short interval of relative moderation between major upheavals in both religion and politics. It was thirteen years after the Declaration of Independence, and the revolutionary passion symbolized by that great document had partly died down. The distrust of government developed during the long struggle with Britain had abated, though it had not disappeared. Almost more important, 1787 was just two years before the outbreak of the French Revolution, which was to bring about in Europe, and for a short time even in America, intense division on basic principles and new, extremely bitter kinds of partisan politics.

1787 was almost a half-century after American society had been divided by the series of fervent religious revivals known as the Great Awakening, and religious passions had cooled down somewhat, though less than some historians have thought. 1787 was a little more than a decade before the Second Great Awakening, that once more shook up and divided not only American religion but American society, profoundly changing its nature. There was still some time to go before the nation felt even the first tremors of romantic democracy, the kind of democracy that used to be associated with Andrew Jackson. 1787 was still part of the eighteenth century;

decorum and sometimes even deference were regarded by many people as virtues. The men who made the Constitution were men of the Enlightenment, that great European movement of thought that told people that they could best understand the universe by trusting the faculties of their own minds. The framers belonged, moreover, to a special early part of the Enlightenment, the moderate, somewhat conservative, mostly English part that had at its heart a strong feeling for balance and order in all things. For all these reasons, 1787 was a time when it was possible—possible though never easy—to reconcile divisions both of interests and ideas by ingenious compromises.

I do not want to present too bland a picture. Not everybody in America was a part of the Moderate Enlightenment. Most historians find that there were important divisions in American thought and society, as there are in all free societies.[1] In the early twentieth century, the days of Charles Beard and Vernon Parrington, people used to talk about the eighteenth century in simple terms—progressives vs. conservatives, believers in liberty vs. believers in order. More recently, historians have had a lot of fun giving new names to much the same groupings: court vs. country; Radical vs. Moderate Whigs, Classical Republicans vs. modern capitalists; the Moderate vs. the Revolutionary Enlightenment; even in religious terms Old vs. New Lights. Perhaps the best words for the two parties are those of J. G. A. Pocock in an early article: the Party of Virtue and the Party of Commerce.[2] Of course everybody at the Convention believed in *both* virtue and commerce, both liberty and order. The difference was over the question what came first right now. To use Pocock's terms, the Party of Virtue consisted of those who put a maximum of individual liberty first, right now and always; who believed in simple republican virtue and were certain that luxury always brought moral, religious, and political decline; who were dubious about the advantages of commerce and not much concerned about foreign affairs; who believed, finally, that the only really trustworthy people were land-owning farmers. These were represented only by a minority of the Philadelphia delegates. The majority in Philadelphia belonged to the Party of Commerce, which means that they believed that right now the most important thing was to make a government that could govern, that could solve the pressing problems of finance, commerce, and foreign policy, of course and always without destroying liberty. Most of the framers believed that the Revolutionary passion for liberty had gone too far in the direction of anarchy, and that this might some day bring a reaction in the direction of tyranny. What emerged in the debates was something of a consensus of moderate conservatives. My purpose in the rest of this talk is to sketch the nature of this consensus, and finally to suggest some of its strengths and weaknesses.

In my opinion the moderately conservative consensus at the Convention arose from basic agreement on the following major topics: religion, human nature, theory of knowledge, political theory, history, and the right kind of governing class. First religion: the Constitution, as has often been pointed out with approval and disapproval, is a remarkably secular document. Unlike the Declaration of Independence, it does not invoke the laws of Nature and of Nature's God, or express a firm reliance on the protection of Divine Providence. This does not mean that the framers were atheists or skeptics. The apparent religious neutrality was partly because some of the framers—especially James Madison—firmly respected America's unique religious diversity and deeply opposed any hint of coercion in religious matters. It was also, I think, because the framers belonged to that section of American opinion—probably a minority but a large one—that distrusted popular emotion and most of all popular religious emotion. People like these—people of the Moderate Enlightenment—believed that religion, like everything else, should speak rather quietly and in reasonable tones. Religious manifestoes had no place in political documents. Most of the framers were deists, Episcopalians, or conservative Presbyterians and Congregationalists—not Baptists, Methodists, or any kind of popular revivalists.[3] All believed in a universe that was presided over by a benevolent deity, a universe that made sense in human terms and was intelligible to human reason. Indeed most if not all the framers would have found it impossible to imagine any other kind of universe.[4] The balanced, intelligible Newtonian order of the cosmos, established by the deity to rule the relation of the sun and the planets, was for the delegates, as for all educated Englishmen, a settled matter, almost a part of their religious faith. In the Convention debates the relation between the federal union and the several states is repeatedly compared to that between the sun and the planets. Few delegates I suspect had a strong belief in special Divine interference in human affairs. At one point in the Convention debates Gouverneur Morris reminded his fellow delegates that they were but men, and could expect no particular Divine intervention to help them.[5] God had done enough by establishing the Law of Nature, from which our rights and duties, Madison and Hamilton both insisted, were derived.[6] Yet, Madison later concluded, in some general and indefinable way, no doubt working through his human servants and not directly, God must have watched over the Convention as He had over the preceding Revolution.[7]

The delegates tended to agree in their ideas about

human nature. Few agreed with their many ultra-Calvinist fellow citizens that humanity was totally depraved. Perhaps as few agreed with Thomas Jefferson, absent in France, on humanity's essential goodness. Almost all would have known, and most would have approved, the balance struck on this matter by Alexander Pope, one of the authors most widely read in the former colonies:

> Virtuous and Vicious ev'ry Man must be,
> Few in th' extreme, but all in the degree; ...

The human mind was for eighteenth-century thinkers a bundle of separate faculties, which checked each other much as the separate parts of the new government were expected to check each other.[8] Among these were interest, passion, reason, and virtue. Much of the time men were governed by selfish interests and by passion. These were, however, balanced, especially among the judicious minority, by virtue and reason. For good government it was necessary to do everything to harness interest and passion to benign ends, and to stimulate and promote reason and virtue.

The founders also agreed in their theory of knowledge, their idea of how the mind actually did its work. They were at once rationalists and empiricists. That is, they believed that human beings can deduce some important principles, especially moral principles, by reasoning directly from axioms that are intuitively known. Most political judgments, however, should be made on the basis of the known facts of human experience. In their theory of knowledge, a contemporary philosopher finds—I am sure correctly—that these men of action were a bit confused.[9] Now, having studied the human mind intensely for two hundred years, we are still confused about how it works. Do you know anybody who is not?

In the science to which the framers appealed most often, the science of government, they argued from a broad consensus. They had read the same books. They drew their political theory first of all from the classics, from Aristotle, Polybius, Cicero, and others. They occasionally mentioned Machiavelli, seldom other thinkers of the Italian Renaissance. More often they cited the European theorists of the past couple of centuries, Grotius, Vattel, Pufendorf, Burlamaqui. Most often of all they appealed to certain major figures of the Moderate Enlightenment—to the illustrious Montesquieu, to British legal authorities like Blackstone, to John Locke the father of liberalism, to David Hume the patron of modernity and moderation, to the contemporary group of Scottish philosophers of common sense.

From this old and cumulative tradition, sometimes recently called the tradition of civic humanism, the framers and people like them had learned that there were three kinds of government: monarchy, aristocracy, and democracy. Each had its strong points and its dangers, its possibility of corruption. Right now monarchy, for Americans, was discredited, and few delegates wanted to establish in America anything much like a real aristocracy. But nothing was more common in the Convention than expressed dislike and fear of pure democracy, of levelling, of the oppression of the few by the many, of the turbulence and folly of the mob. A few delegates, starting with James Wilson and the aged Benjamin Franklin, argued stoutly for a large *element* of democracy in the new government, pointing to the heroic actions of the people during the war and suggesting that it would be both dangerous and unfair to take back powers that people had already gained. But all agreed that whatever democratic elements there were going to be in the new government, these needed to be qualified and controlled.

More than to any kind of theory the delegates appealed to history, including both their reading and their experience. This has led some to conclude that these were practical men, men to whom ideas mattered little. Yet nobody can look at history and experience except through the eyes of some sort of theory, least of all those who express contempt for theory as the delegates never did. Historians have gradually come to admit that everybody looks at history from a point of view (a shocking statement when Charles Beard made it long ago). They even admit this about historians—especially *other* historians. When the Philadelphia delegates looked at history they started by accepting the prevailing belief that human nature was constant and unchanging in all periods, and that therefore classical precedents were absolutely relevant to contemporary problems. They were clearly not economic determinists. Not being fools, they knew that concrete interests played a big part in determining human actions. Not being cynics either, they believed that these interests could be counterbalanced by virtue and reason. In their arguments in favor of balanced government they appealed constantly to history—to the experience of Greece and Rome, to all European attempts at confederation, to the experience of the existing republics of Holland and Switzerland, and to the recently destroyed republican monarchy of Poland. They appealed much more often to the long experience of constitutional government in Britain, as this was interpreted by some rather peculiar contemporary theorists. Finally they appealed to their own experience of government in America, making use of the wonderful political laboratory afforded by thirteen separate political structures.

There was one more source of agreement, often tacit but sometimes expressed, the assumptions of the delegates about class differences. Of course the political class was limited to white males, but not all white males were believed to be equally capable of carrying on the business of government. Self-evident truth, most of the framers believed, was much more self-evident to some than to others. On the whole government worked best if it remained in the hands of gentlemen of generous education and large views. Usually this meant men of some property, and, some added, of established family. Most hoped there would be more mobility in America than in Europe. People should be able to move upward into the governing class, but only by education, industry, and the resulting acquisition of property. People without property were to be distrusted, as were those whose view was confined to narrow local matters. Worst of all were unscrupulous demagogues, who appealed to the passions of the mob. The framers were quite frank about all this; after all they were talking to each other behind closed doors. This kind of assumption, together with all the other theoretical and practical sources of agreement, led gradually during the long hot summer to the emergence of a working consensus that can be expressed in a few axioms:

First, the purpose of government everywhere and always is to establish and protect liberty. Second, there can be no liberty without order, and no liberty *or* order without property. Third, since men are unequal in ability, there will always be inequality of property, though it is to be hoped that this will be less flagrant here than in Europe. Fourth, since there will thus always be a few and a many, the job of government is to protect each against the other. Fifth, for this and other reasons, there must be separation of powers. So far all was familiar, but now comes the Convention's great imaginative leap.

Since there are not in America any separate orders, no king and no hereditary nobility, balance must be achieved even while the whole government rests ultimately on the people. This means, among other things, that each branch must be chosen in a different way and that the President, Senate, and House must be chosen by separate electorates.

Another way to understand the intellectual consensus that had led to this clever conclusion is to ask what the framers did *not* believe. Assumptions and ideas that would have seemed to them impossible and probably unintelligible include the following: That the universe is completely random or unknowable. That people today can never really understand the past. That government is not concerned with liberty, only with order and efficiency. That morality is irrelevant to government. That you can have liberty without private property. That all people are equally good and wise. That the heart is a better source of understanding than the head,[10] that instinct is better than education. It is very instructive to realize that many people today believe each of these axioms. There may well be nobody reading this essay who rejects all of them.

How then are we to judge this document under which we have lived so long, this document which comes to us from an intellectual world entirely different from our own? To begin with, we must realize that the Constitution has changed very drastically since 1787. It was changed in the process of ratification. The other side of the divided Revolutionary tradition, the side that put a maximum of individual liberty first and distrusted all government, the Party of Virtue, fought vigorously against the adoption of the Constitution on democratic and libertarian grounds, and insisted successfully on the addition of a Bill of Rights. The Constitution has been amended mainly in a democratic direction. The election of Senators by state legislatures has gone; the meaning of the electoral college has changed. After a terrible war the compromises about slavery have been destroyed. After long struggles both blacks and women have been added to the electorate. Political parties, detested by the framers, were found very early to be essential to the practical operation of the Constitution. The greatest single democratic triumph at the Convention, the provision for the admission of new and equal states, has changed the Constitution in the way conservatives feared. Most of all, the meaning of the Constitution has been changed by the changing environment, physical and political, national and global. If they could see our America the framers would certainly be baffled, and in some ways horrified. Exactly the things they feared—huge cities, extreme wealth and poverty, an immensely powerful military establishment, have come into being. They spoke for a world to which we can never return—and despite our occasional nostalgia few of us would like it if we could.

What is surprising, however, is how much remains of the eighteenth century in our Constitution. No wonder foreign commentators are baffled by this country, the country of innovation and democracy, which still lives under a basic document that embodies many of the ideas, beliefs, and fears of the Moderate Enlightenment. To live under such a document as a great power in the modern world is, we all know, not easy. Our Constitutional tradition has both advantages and disadvantages. It has worked well, again and again, just as the founders hoped it would, in preventing tyranny, in preserving liberty against threats from the executive and legislative branches—against power grabs, coups, and juntas. It has so far made impossible the development even in wartime of military government, the type of government most detested by the framers. It has usually proved a wonderful instrument for reconciling hostilities and achieving compromise.

It has also had the faults that go with its great virtues. It is eternally frustrating to those who believe that a dynamic, activist government is necessary in the modern world. It has made things very difficult for those who believe in a foreign policy of intervention and world power. Its genius for conciliation and compromise breaks down when issues arise that are irreconcilable, that arouse all-out loyalty and strong emotions on both sides. The most tragic example of this of course is the Civil War, when each side was sure that it was not only morally superior but more loyal to the Constitution than its enemy. Other irreconcilable differences may arise—perhaps the one that looms biggest on the horizon right now is abortion.

As the Moderate Enlightenment knew so well—here agreeing with its Calvinist opponents—nothing human can be perfect. We are quite right to celebrate the Constitution, to be grateful for its protection, to be proud of a long record of ordered liberty. But nothing could be less appropriate to the spirit in which the Constitution was made—the spirit of the Moderate Enlightenment—than uncritical adulation. The Constitution was made by fallible men who knew they were fallible. Thomas Jefferson, who was certainly a man of the Enlightenment, sometimes Moderate but sometimes Radical, was not in Philadelphia in 1787 but in Paris. When he read the document, at first he had serious doubts about it. He worried particularly about the dangerous power of the President. As his friend Madison explained the document to him, Jefferson soon came to approve it, and eventually to admire it deeply. Still later, when he was President, he chafed under some of its restraints like all strong presidents. This is his evaluation, in a letter of 1816, of the whole work of the generation of founding fathers:

> I knew that age well; I belonged to it, and labored with it. It deserved well of its country. It was very like the present, but without the experience of the present and forty years of experience in government is worth a century of book-reading; and this they would say themselves, were they to rise from the dead.[11]

Later, in 1835, Alexis de Tocqueville, the most astute foreign observer of the United States, rated the framers of the Constitution much more highly:

> At the time when it was formed, the ruin of the Confederation seemed imminent, and its danger was universally known. In this extremity the people chose the men who most deserved their esteem rather than those who had gained the affections of the country.... Distinguished as almost all the legislators of the union were for their intelligence, they were still more so for their patriotism.... They had the courage to say what they believed to be true, because they were animated by a warm and sincere love of liberty; and they ventured to propose restrictions [of liberty] because they were resolutely opposed to destruction [of it].[12]

That is still pretty much in the spirit of the Moderate Enlightenment, a tradition that this French aristocratic liberal thoroughly admired. Some other and more general advice of Tocqueville may be more useful to us, here and today. He tells us how we should look at the past, including the great generation of the founders:

> We have not to seek to make ourselves like our progenitors, but to strive to work out that species of greatness and happiness which is our own.[13]

7

The Enlightenment and America: The Jeffersonian Moment

This was written for a conference on the Virginia Statute of Religious Liberty, held at Charlottesville, Virginia, 1985. It is reprinted by permission of the Virginia Foundation for the Humanities and Public Policy.

The Enlightenment, according to several important historians, was developed in Europe and put into practice in America.[1] In my opinion, this statement is not and could not possibly be true. How could a set of ideas, deeply rooted in two thousand years of European intellectual history, be transferred intact to a new continent and a new society? And did the Enlightenment have a program of action? It had many.

One must at this point at least try to answer two obvious questions: Did the Enlightenment exist? and if so What was it? My answer to the first question is emphatically yes.[2] Whether one defines it as an ideology, a party, a style, or a mood, the Enlightenment is a recognizable phenomenon of the late seventeenth and eighteenth centuries. People consciously experienced it then; historians recognized it later.

The phenomenon, however, is so diverse that it is difficult to formulate a definition that will stick. The Enlightenment was not necessarily, for instance, optimistic.[3] It was not always rationalistic. It was not always empirical or pragmatic in method. About the only common content that I have been able to find can be put in two very simple statements: First, by definition the Enlightenment consisted of those who believed that the present age was in some sense more enlightened than the past, that people had become better able to understand the universe. Second, Enlightened people believed that this understanding was best achieved through the use of the natural faculties of the human mind, and not by reliance on either revelation or mystical illumination. Only on the basis of these propositions, I believe, and not any social or political program, is it possible to bring together such very different people with very different political ideas as Hume and Paine, Voltaire, Condorcet, and Jefferson. And who would exclude any of these from the canon of the Enlightenment?

The Enlightenment through most of its European development was incompatible with two major forces shaping early American culture: the first, social and political democracy; the second, evangelical Protestantism. The conflict with these two forces greatly limited the effect of the Enlightenment in America. It is surprising that it nonetheless left important effects on American politics and culture. My thesis today is that most of the triumphs of the Enlightenment in America were achieved in a relatively short period, roughly the last quarter of the eighteenth century, a time I shall call the Jeffersonian moment.

Let me first discuss briefly the difficult relations between the Enlightenment on one side and the two shaping forces I have mentioned, democracy and Protestantism. If one uses the word "democracy" about the society of late eighteenth-century America one must use it in a distinctly relative sense. Certainly the new nation was not the simple egalitarian Utopia imagined by some Enlightened Europeans. And yet—always with the major and fateful exception of the black slaves—America was more egalitarian than any European country, and it was changing at an accelerated pace in an egalitarian direction. Political participation was broader in America, and habits of social deference were far weaker.

The Enlightenment on the other hand was deeply rooted in two thousand years of a culture that took for granted the existence and necessity of different social orders. From the ancient world, filtered through the Renaissance, the Enlightenment drew its assumption, sometimes stated clearly and sometimes taken for granted, that society must be directed by the educated, and that meant the classically educated. Professor Pocock has illuminated the transition through the Renaissance to the seventeenth and eighteenth centuries of the political ideas of Aristotle and Polybius. To educated Europeans, democracy was one of the three possible forms of government, each with its vices and virtues. This left open wide possibilities for practical choices. In England, Enlightened thinkers tended to believe that the best government was the one that best achieved a balance among the one, the few, and the many. In France, many of the philosophes believed that in practice an Enlightened despot was most likely to carry out the program devised by Enlightened intellectuals. Voltaire and others found themselves happy and at home at the courts of Frederick and Catherine.

Whatever their political preferences, Enlightened thinkers found it very hard to believe that the masses could play any major part in shaping the social order or governing the society. Social reform might be directed toward their improvement, but the direction must be defined from above. It seems to me very revealing that in French there is no single word for the Enlightenment, one must say the age of the *Lumières,* of the bright lights, the stars, the geniuses. A recent French book on the Enlightenment asks a startling question: "Did not the Europe of the Enlightenment (l'Europe des Lumières) inherit the *imperium romanum?* Like the ancient Roman world, it gives off a feeling of civilization surrounded by barbarism."[4] When Enlightened thinkers spoke of the masses, they sometimes spoke with humane sympathy, sometimes in terms of fear, indifference, even hatred. To many, especially in France, efforts to educate the masses were not only futile but dangerous. "As for the *canaille,*" said Voltaire, "I have no concern with it; it will always remain *canaille.*" "We have never pretended to enlighten shoemakers and servants."[5] This sort of statement could be endlessly duplicated from the writings of Enlightened thinkers. Even Rousseau, for all his emotionally egalitarian tendencies, was sure that the poor had no business with education. These views came not only from past tradition but from looking at present society; resources simply did not exist to enlighten everybody, such a task would at best take a very long time.

The leading spokesmen of the Enlightenment in America differed in part from this pattern. They did not depend on court favor but spoke for a vigorous bourgeois society of which they were part. The masses in a society of small cities with relatively open opportunities were less frightening. Popular Enlightenment could be at least a hope for the future. Yet in America too the founding fathers read European books and drew from them many of the assumptions of the European Enlightenment.

John Adams, among the major figures, followed most closely the political traditions of European thinkers. He detested hereditary monarchy and nobility but tried very hard to find in America a means of balancing the few and the many, if not the one. Since he was frank to the point of provocative bluntness, he got in trouble for this, but stuck to his guns. "Democracy, simple democracy," he insisted, "never had a patron among men of letters,"[6] and he was not far wrong. Madison and his colleagues at Philadelphia tried hard to find a way of providing the traditional kind of balance without resorting to any permanent or unchangeable or hereditary order. Thomas Jefferson spoke a lot and sincerely about his trust in the people. Yet he was sufficiently a man of the Enlightenment to believe that what they could be trusted to do was to choose enlightened gentlemen to govern them. In old age he agreed with Adams that "there is a natural aristocracy among men. . . . May we not even say, that that form of government is best, which provides the most effectually for a pure selection of these natural *aristoi* into the offices of government?"[7] And in practice, his program for public education in Virginia, intended to be a companion piece to the Statute we are celebrating, was directed toward the training of a meritocracy. Its purpose, in Jefferson's memorable phrase, was to see that the best geniuses were "raked from the rubbish," without regard to their families and financial resources.[8]

The preamble of the bill itself says that democratic society can be saved from degeneration only by an elite:

those persons, whom nature hath endowed with genius and virtue, should be rendered by liberal education worthy to receive, and able to guard the sacred deposit of the rights and liberties of their fellow citizens.[9]

This was about as far as the Enlightenment could move in an egalitarian direction.

In my opinion the principal ideological force working toward ideological force working toward ideological egalitarianism in America was radical Protestantism. Like most of the insurrections of the masses against a society of orders all through European history, the discontented in America were likely to draw on the radically egalitarian texts of the New Testament, which seemed to say, in sharp contrast to the teachings of the Enlightened philosophers, that the poor and the simple were wiser than the well-to-do and the carefully educated in what mattered most. This view was broadcast by some of the most effective preachers of the Great Awakening in mid-century. It was the teaching of the fastest-growing religious groups in America before, during, and after the American Revolution and it had a great future in American religion in the nineteenth century. Nothing could be in sharper contrast to the central tenets of the Enlightenment, and spokesmen of Enlightened, liberal religion made this amply clear.

And yet the actual historical relations between the Enlightenment and religion, the Enlightenment and Christianity, and the Enlightenment and Protestantism were all complex, not simple. All the Enlightened thinkers had to define their position in relation to religion; none ignored it. Only a few, mainly French intellectuals of the mid-century, detested all religion and hoped to replace it by some sort of systematic materialism or deepgoing skepticism. Many hoped to replace Christianity with a better and more moral religion, usually deism. Many believed like Voltaire that Christianity, however absurd, would always be necessary to keep the masses in order. Some, less cynical, believed that Christianity could be pruned and purified, reduced to its essentials, reconciled with reason.

The kind of religion hated most by Enlightened philosophers was of course Voltaire's *infâme,* an official church with persecuting powers. Toward radical Protestantism, a world they knew little about, the French philosophes were more likely to be tolerant, baffled, and patronizing. Especially "Les Quakers," associated with simplicity, peace, and friendship toward Indians, got a good press in Paris, though Voltaire says little about their religion except that they wear their hats in church. Spokesmen of the British Enlightenment, on the other hand, whether Latitudinarian or deist were more likely to hate and fear enthusiasts and sectarians. They looked back with horror to the Puritan Commonwealth, and were offended by the vulgarity and noisiness of contemporary Methodists.

Many compromises were possible and many were tried, yet during most of its changing career the Enlightenment could not but be basically hostile to evangelical Protestantism. The deepest loyalties of the Enlightened were affronted by the teaching that divine grace, arbitrarily bestowed by an inscrutable God, was more important than any kind of earthly achievement. They were revolted by statements that most of mankind were and always must be miserable sinners. Those who tried hardest to formulate a modern, rational, Enlightened Christianity were continually at war with preachers who insisted that saving knowledge came only through a change of heart.

Perhaps the central purpose of the Enlightenment was to find a new and rational, essentially a secular basis for knowledge, education, and government. It is significant that Jefferson's bill for the more general diffusion of knowledge provided that children in primary schools should study not Scripture but "Graecian, Roman, English, and American history."[10] The Enlightenment amounted to a gigantic choice between two equal parts of the European cultural heritage. It opted for the classics, clarity, and reason, against the Bible, mystery, and faith.

And yet, against all apparent probability, there was a Jeffersonian moment, in Virginia and in the world, when Enlightenment, radical Protestantism, and democracy seemed to come together in a great revolutionary alliance. Part of this came from a change, beginning about 1760 and quickening for the next thirty years, in the nature of the Enlightenment itself. I have tried to explain how the British Enlightenment of moderation and compromise, the largely French Enlightenment of skepticism and cynicism, began in the later part of the century to be displaced by a new Revolutionary Enlightenment.[11] Science and education, said the Revolutionary Enlightenment, could produce a new world. Irrational privilege, cruel punishments, slavery, arbitrary government, and religious oppression could all soon be ended as reason spread from the Enlightened minority—not perhaps to everybody but in ever wider circles. In a recent review, J. H. Plumb defends the accomplishments of this kind of Enlightenment against some powerful traducers, and attempts to give it a social base. He speaks of

> . . . the beneficial social revolution brought about at that time by a combination of capitalist enterprise, technological inventions, scientific understanding, and a deep social confidence among the petty bourgeoisie. What was new in the late eighteenth century was not the misery, the evil, or the exploitation, but the spreading sense in America, Britain, and Europe that men could change their earthly destiny,

that they could master nature as well as politics. Naive, perhaps, and doomed to terrible disappointment, but at its birth social hope was intoxicating.[12]

Complicated people turned toward a belief in simplicity. If we must use the labels given diverse currents of thought by historians of ideas—and I do not see how we can get along without them—the Enlightenment began to drift in the direction of Romanticism, with Jean-Jacques Rousseau poised precariously in the rapids, Godwin and Shelley clear over the falls.

One of the most important causes and results of this change was a temporary alliance between the Enlightenment and Protestant Christianity. Recently a whole string of excellent scholars has rediscovered the millennial side of Protestant teaching, and pointed out how much there was in common between the biblical and secular reactions of a new golden age.[13] For some Protestants especially, the thousand years of peace and justice seemed to be about to dawn, possibly unaccompanied by cataclysm. For some Enlightened philosophers, a new era of peace and justice was about to be achieved through some sort of rational and moderate revolution.

In England, it can never be forgotten, Whigs were almost necessarily Protestants. It was sometimes true that Radical Whigs were Radical Protestants. The historians of the Commonwealth tradition have pointed out brilliantly the survival into the eighteenth century of the traditions of Milton and Sidney, the hate of corruption and oppression, the longing for simplicity and justice. Sometimes, I think, they have not given sufficient emphasis to the temporary radicalization of English dissent in the late eighteenth century, following its failure to secure the removal of dissenters' disabilities by Parliament.[14]

As we all have learned, Radical Whig theory was especially popular in the New World, and not only in New England with its glowing memories of the seventeenth-century Cromwellian Commonwealth. The two individuals who best incarnate the Whig-Dissenter-American alliance were two great friends of Thomas Jefferson—Richard Price and Joseph Priestley. Both were Radical Whigs and ultra-liberal Protestants. Both were in their way men of the Enlightenment, believers in science and progress. Both were militant defenders of the American Revolution. With little or no friction they were able to ally themselves with Thomas Paine, who came from a dissenting background. In his American revolutionary propaganda Paine quoted Scripture with apparent deep respect, appealing from the royal brute of Great Britain to the king who reigns above. Ultra-Calvinists, liberal Christians, and deists were able to submerge their differences in the Glorious Cause of the American Revolution.[15]

The summit of the new kind of Enlightenment came with the early period of the French Revolution, greeted with rapture and millennial hope by Priestley, with revolutionary enthusiasm by Paine, with a somewhat more sober kind of joy by Price and Jefferson. If one wants a particular date for the climax of the Jeffersonian moment, it might be 1789, when Jefferson sailed for home, confident that he left behind a new France which had managed to end feudal privileges, secure freedom of speech and religion, and establish a limited monarchy suitable for the needs of the only partly Enlightened population. Jefferson was glad he had been able to play a role—a role which he did not exaggerate—as a disinterested adviser on Enlightened revolution. Now he was quite willing to leave all this to the French and return to America, the real homeland of liberty and progress, and especially to his own country, Virginia.

In that commonwealth a great deal had been going
on since Jefferson left. It is not my purpose to describe
or analyze the Virginian struggle that culminated in the
Statute for Religious Liberty. What I want to do is to
locate this crucial local struggle in the history of the
Enlightenment, and particularly in the beginning of the
revolutionary phase of the Enlightenment, the time I am
describing as the Jeffersonian moment. Jefferson himself, despite his fervent hopes, was enough a man of the
classical tradition to see the danger of the declining Po-
lybian cycle. He perceived the end of the Revolutionary
War as a brief propitious moment, and it was with this
in mind that he introduced his program for the reform
of the laws and institutions of Virginia.

> the spirit of the times may alter, will alter. Our rulers will
> become corrupt, our people careless. A single zealot may
> commence persecution, and better men be his victims. It
> can never be too often repeated, that the time for fixing
> every essential right on a legal basis is while our rulers are
> honest, and ourselves united. From the conclusion of this
> war we shall be going down hill. . . . The shackles, therefore,
> which shall not be knocked off at the conclusion of this war,
> will remain on us long, will be made heavier and heavier,
> till our rights shall revive or expire in a convulsion.[16]

Now was the time, therefore, to put the axe to the root
of landed aristocracy, to rationalize the laws, to provide
a gradual end to slavery, and to secure forever religious
freedom.

This last great objective was the central—but not the
only—objective of Jefferson; in his whole plan to change
his beloved Virginia this was his only major and permanent victory. We know that this victory depended on
an alliance very similar to that which had won the Revolutionary struggle in the nation as a whole. In Virginia

this alliance took the form of a combination between deists and radical Protestants against a battered and weakened establishment.[17] We now give full credit to the contribution of James Madison, mediating with consummate skill among Baptists, Presbyterians, and liberal Anglicans, putting through the Statute while Jefferson was in Paris.

The troops were Baptists and Presbyterians and the tactics were Madison's, but the words—with a few minor corrections made by the Assembly—were Jefferson's. These words were and are wholly representative of the early and most hopeful stage of the Revolutionary Enlightenment. In his description of the Statute in "Notes on Virginia," Jefferson, at this time a sincere deist and later a special sort of rational and Unitarian Christian, allowed himself a couple of sentences that were to be used by his enemies for the rest of his life to indict him for indifference to religion:

> The legitimate powers of government extend to such acts only as are injurious to others. But it does me no injury for my neighbor to say there are twenty gods, or no God. It neither picks my pocket nor breaks my leg.[18]

The preamble to the Statute itself is more conciliatory. It is mainly an extremely eloquent statement of intellectual liberty, and it makes some use of the argument that coercion is harmful to religion itself. This argument had been stressed continually by Madison in the long legislative struggle. Almighty God has made the mind free and the "holy author of our religion" decided against coercion and (in Jefferson's original draft) in favor of propagating the truth by reason alone. It is significant, however, that Madison managed to defeat an amendment making it clear that the holy author mentioned was

Jesus Christ. Jefferson regarded this particular victory as making it clear that the protection of the law was extended to "the Jew and the Gentile, the Christian and Mahometan, the Hindoo, and infidel of every denomination."[19] It is clear too that both Madison and Jefferson saw the religious freedom declared in the Statute as extending well beyond religion strictly defined. Jefferson's original text carried the phrase, deleted by the Assembly, "that the opinions of men are not the object of civil government, nor under its jurisdiction," and Madison, informing Jefferson of the victory, believed that the enacting clauses "have in this country extinguished for ever the ambitious hope of making laws for the human mind."[20] And Jefferson clearly intended the Statute to play a major part in the worldwide spread of the new kind of Enlightenment. He and others, including Richard Price, saw to it that the act of the Virginia Assembly received the widest possible circulation in France, where it was much admired, together with the Declaration of Independence and the Virginia Bill of Rights.[21]

The Jeffersonian moment was precisely that time in which it was possible to believe that the program of the Revolutionary Enlightenment would be carried out in Virginia, the United States, and then Europe. We know now that this happened nowhere. Most of Jefferson's program for Virginia, including the revision of the laws, the program for graduated and Enlightened education, and the program for the gradual abolition of slavery, was either defeated or abandoned. Despite some important Jeffersonian victories still to come, one can hardly say that the United States itself became a model Enlightened republic, administered in the interest of all by the wisest and best educated. And the course of revolution in Europe was about to move in a direction that permanently separated it from its American wellwishers.

The Jeffersonian moment was in considerable part a matter of timing. The Virginian struggle and its one great victory came about, as Jefferson said, in the glow of successful revolution, and before the revolutionary scene was altered by a number of historical developments of the end of the century. These can be summarized either in terms of political history or in terms of religious history, and I should like to attempt briefly first one and then the other kind of summary.

In political terms, according to an interesting recent article by Gordon Wood, Enlightened political leadership like that of the founding fathers was made forever impossible by a process of democratization, extending from the struggle over the Constitution through the fierce party battles of the 1790s. Wood by no means entirely deplores or regrets this change:

> For in the end what made subsequent duplication of the remarkable intellectual leadership of the Revolutionaries impossible in America was the growth of what we have come to value most—egalitarian culture and our democratic society. One of the prices we had to pay for democracy was a decline in the intellectual quality of American political life and an eventual separation between ideas and power.[22]

Joyce Appleby sees a similar process, regarding it with more enthusiasm. Democratic politics and burgeoning capitalism produced in the 1790s a new kind of republican ideology displacing elitist classical republicanism.[23] She regards the Jeffersonian victory in 1800 as "the single most important change in the history of American political culture." It was seen at the time by many, including Joseph Priestley, as the dawn of a new age of hope and freedom. Yet Jefferson in power, trying hard to conciliate his enemies, refrained from introducing a concrete program of Enlightened reform like that he had hoped for in Virginia. He gave little support to his radical supporters who wanted a complete revision of the laws on an Enlightened mode.[24] He refrained from pushing Joel Barlow's program of systematic government support of the arts and sciences on the ground that the public would not support it.[25] And as President he did nothing to disturb the institution of slavery.

Ever more inclined to mediate and compromise, Enlightened Virginians held onto the presidency for the rest of the dynasty. The last President brought up in the Enlightenment was John Quincy Adams, trained in Europe by both his father and Jefferson, defeated partly because he proposed a program, a very un-revolutionary program to be sure, for national support of science and education. John Quincy Adams, for all his many virtues, was no Jefferson. Another way of looking at the change in the nature of political leadership in America is to realize that in the nineteenth century it became impossible for anybody, even a Jefferson, even a Goethe, to combine knowledge of the classics, of political theory, of the arts and sciences with the art of government. Both culture and politics had become too complicated and various to be controlled by an Enlightened statesman. Perhaps they always had been.

Part of the caution of Jefferson and his immediate successors arose from the involvement of the United States in the worldwide struggles growing out of the French Revolution. Reluctantly, later than many, but very completely, Jefferson abandoned his confidence in the French Republic. Writing sadly to Lafayette in 1815 he concluded that the fault had lain with those who pushed the Revolution too far, abandoning their constitutional monarchy for "the unprincipled and bloody tyranny of Robespierre, and the equally unprincipled and maniac tyranny of Bonaparte."[26] Jefferson's picture of Napoleon is as hostile as Tolstoy's. It is ironic that Napoleon, sacrificing freedom, put over in France some parts of the program of the Revolutionary Enlightenment, including a systematic revision of the laws and a systematic support of the arts and sciences. The different choices made at this time have separated European and American culture ever since. More and more, in his old age, Jefferson abandoned the universalistic hopes of his youth and became convinced that America was the world's only hope. Yet even in America, he wrote John Taylor in 1816, government was not as republican as he had hoped and expected:

> the people have less regular control over their agents, than their rights and their interests require. . . . Much I apprehend that the golden moment is past for reforming these heresies.[27]

The end of the Jeffersonian moment can also be described in terms of religious history. Paine's *Age of Reason* in 1795 brought into the field a new kind of deism, popular, missionary, and absolutely unsparing of religious feelings and prejudices. Jefferson, who on principle kept his religious opinions to himself, was acceptable as an ally to some kinds of evangelical Protestants; Paine could be only an enemy. The next major sign of change was the counter-offensive of the New England orthodox establishment against Jefferson and all other spokesmen of all varieties of the Enlightenment. The orthodox campaign failed politically and damaged its sponsors, but it did mean that throughout the nineteenth century Paine, Voltaire, Hume, Volney, and others became symbols of atheism and Jacobinism, frightening and foreign, to millions of American Prot-

estants. Finally, and most important, was the other Revolution of 1800, the religious revival that changed the
nature of American society and religion, leaving it as
different from New England Puritanism as it was from
Virginian Enlightenment. For the rest of the century, I
think it is fair to say, most Americans believed at the
same time that man was a sinner dependent on unmer-
ited grace and that he was endowed with the right and
ability to govern himself. Anybody who can understand
this paradox—if there is anybody—can claim to understand nineteenth-century America.

Nineteenth-century America—that strange and formidable culture—could never have been predicted, approved, or understand by any prophet of the eighteenth-
century Enlightenment. This is true whether one emphasizes emotional and populist politics, emotional and
militant religion, secular and semi-secular Romanticism,
the spread of slavery and of militant antislavery, or the
growth of industrialism and mass culture. As for the
America of the twentieth century, of television, world
war, and nuclear terror, to see all this as in some manner
the carrying out of the program of the Enlightenment
needs an act of faith which few can manage. The program of the Enlightenment was carried out nowhere.

This may seem a somber conclusion for what is rightly
to be seen as a celebratory occasion. Perhaps it is: in the
present un-Jeffersonian moment I see little function for
complacency. And at no time does either self-congrat-
ulation or nostalgia form any part of the business of the
historian.

I certainly do not mean to say or imply that nineteenth-century America was, or that twentieth-century
America is, worse in every way than the actuality—as
opposed to the hopes—of the eighteenth century. Hopes
and dreams and programs, never carried through ex-

actly, yet have their important place in history. From the various kinds of Enlightenment, some things survived into a different world. From early and relatively conservative forms of Enlightenment thought, which carried within them the heritage of the classics, we got our eighteenth-century Constitution, with its magnificent defense in the Federalist Papers. And from the Revolutionary Enlightenment, from the Jeffersonian moment when Enlightenment, democracy, and Protestantism briefly came together, we inherit among other things the Statute we are celebrating and its national amplification, the Bill of Rights. It is in terms of religious liberty that we have come closest to carrying through one of the planks of the Radical Enlightenment's platform, though with consequences far different from those Jefferson and his friends expected. Religious freedom led in the nineteenth century to the great triumph of evangelical Protestantism, and in the twentieth to the survival, in America more than in any other advanced country, of traditional religious beliefs.

Perhaps most important of all in the heritage of the Revolutionary Enlightenment are words: the great words that any country needs to embody its best hopes. The Declaration of Independence has been invoked by every movement that has tried to make this a better country, including those that have struggled to carry its traditions into new spheres. Among these are the movement for racial equality, a problem that stumped Jefferson, or sexual equality, a program beyond most eighteenth-century imaginations. And the great words of the Statute we are celebrating survive as a major weapon every time government or any faction attempts to curtail religious liberty.

8

After the Enlightenment:
A Prospectus

This essay, written especially for this volume, deals with a transition that has long intrigued me. Perhaps it also serves to link together the topics treated in this volume. In working on it, I received very helpful comments from my friends Ruth Bloch, Charles Capper, Daniel Howe, James Kettner, Fred and Jean Matthews, and Robert Middlekauff.

I have long been haunted by a remark made by the late John William Ward, in his *Andrew Jackson: Symbol for an Age* (1955). The book explains that Jackson was presented by his political admirers as an example of the intuitive wisdom of the people, always to be preferred to the arid and bookish rationalism of people like Jackson's opponent, John Quincy Adams. The passage that intrigues me is this:

> The attitude that underlies Jacksonian democracy can best be expressed in terms made current in American by New England Transcendentalism. The conjunction of Jackson and anything connected with New England may at first seem inappropriate, but the Jacksonians not only grappled

with the same problem as the Transcendentalists (in different terms, perhaps) but arrived at a similar answer.[1]

Western editors and politicians who had never heard of Schelling or Coleridge used the same arguments as New England intellectuals, who were steeped in these authors, feared Jackson, and usually voted for his opponents. Both of these sharply contrasting groups believed that divine truth was to be found deep within the consciousness of all men, and that the inner self was in touch with—indeed was part of—nature and God. Both had harsh things to say about too much dependence on books, on learning, on dry syllogistic reasoning.

Ward does not try to tell us *why* these ideas had quite suddenly spread so widely in many forms and on many intellectual levels. The nearest thing to a hint he gives us comes near the end of his book, where he says that Jackson, as symbol, "was the creation of the times."[2] Here he seems to be talking about an irresistible time-spirit, the well-known Zeitgeist of old-fashioned Romantic historians. This was a concept long unfashionable when Ward was writing, partly because of its sometimes ugly political associations. Yet few scholars then or now would deny that some major intellectual and emotional change was going on all over the European world in the late eighteenth and early nineteenth century. In talking about this change we still have to use the old shorthand: the world was moving from something called the Enlightenment to something called Romanticism. Speaking of this great change in terms of America alone, and primarily in terms of political thought, Gordon Wood has made a ringing claim for its importance:

> This vast transformation, this move from classical republicanism to romantic democracy in a matter of decades, was

the real American revolution, creating for many Americans a cultural crisis as severe as any in American history.[3]

It is impossible to explain completely any change this large and complex, yet to illuminate such transformations is perhaps the most important as well as the most difficult assignment for a historian. There is as yet no first-rate book on the whole movement in American culture from the Enlightenment to Romanticism, though many fascinating suggestions have been made ever since those of Perry Miller. Recently much fine work has been done, both in old and new kinds of history, that illuminates one or another aspect of this major cultural shift. Perhaps it is time to begin to think about a synthesis. This essay is a tentative effort in that direction.

Any historian who deals with the decline of the Enlightenment in America must begin by bearing in mind that this was an international development. The Enlightenment was an eighteenth-century European movement, the culmination of a cultural history going very consciously back to the ancients. It did not endure far into the nineteenth century in any country. Of course many important legacies remained and from time to time new versions of the Enlightenment were proclaimed. Some of these much-revised nineteenth-century versions of the Enlightenment survived better in continental Europe than in either England or America, though the Enlightenment had begun in England and many philosophes tried hard to see the United States as the country of the Enlightenment *par excellence*.

Explanations of the end of the Enlightenment in Europe are of three major kinds. The first comes from the intellectual history of the movement itself. The Enlightenment was severely challenged from within. Hume and then Kant challenged its most basic assertion: that moral judgments can be made on the basis of factual information. A whole string of philosophers, from then to now, have continued to sustain this denial, and to demonstrate that one cannot derive "ought from is."[4]

The second kind of explanation, more recently developed and more tentative, comes from the historians of popular religion, popular literature, and popular culture in general. It is possible to argue that the prevailing tone of the Enlightened authors, cool and rational and restrained, never really satisfied some kinds of human needs. The great originator of this emotional attack on the Enlightenment is of course Rousseau, who began his long career of shocking statements by denying one of the Enlightenment's most basic assertions: that people are made happier by intellectual advance. Thousands in every country wept over Rousseau's novels, and many imitated them. Some tried hard to follow Rousseau's liberating but illusory principles in raising and educating their children.

This argument is often closely related to the third kind of explanation, which comes from social history. The Enlightenment depended on the perception by its adherents that human culture and society were becoming more orderly and predictable. This had never been the experience of European peasants, the majority of the population, a group that had never been much affected anywhere by the Enlightenment. Most of the philosophes, even their most articulate and passionate modern admirer concedes, never developed a program for what many of them called the *canaille*.[5] Voltaire was confident that this did not matter, while his more penetrating contemporary, Diderot, worried about the lack.[6] Even the more optimistic of the philosophes assumed, consciously or not, that the world would remain stable during the long period it would take for the people to be educated.

The two great events of the era, the French and Industrial Revolution, ended the complacency of European intellectuals.[7] The French Revolution made it essential, once and for all, for all social thinkers, radicals and reactionaries alike, to have *some* sort of program for the masses. The industrial revolution, gathering its strength more gradually, shifted power to new classes and demanded new kinds of virtues. In many different ways, and on many levels, the nineteenth century put a premium on dynamism rather than stability, expansion rather than classical restraint, sentiment or even passion rather than rationality.

The same winds were blowing in America, but their effects were partly different. At the end of the eighteenth century a number of major developments—religious, socio-economic, and political—were at work changing America and increasing its difference from Europe.

The first of these to be apparent was religious revival. An essentially constant and always powerful Protestant religiosity was confirmed, expanded, and altered by the Great Revival beginning at about the turn of the century. It left American religion even more different from European than it had always been—looser, more various, and above all more popular. In Europe, many devoted members of the clergy and laity tried hard to revive religion, often with considerable success. Yet the European churches were never entirely able to break their connection with the old regime. This problem did not exist in America, where the major churches had been formed in opposition to authority.

A little later, the American economy and society were affected by all the changes associated with the increasingly rapid development of a market economy. First, a large-scale agriculture was developed for export during the Napoleonic Wars. Second, a promising industrial growth dotted the Eastern landscape with textile mills and iron smelters. What was unique about American capitalist development was its continental theater. Internal exchanges and a rapidly growing home market brought the possibility of something approaching self-sufficiency. More and more, prosperity and expansion were linked with divine Providence and political freedom in American ideology. Whatever power had once been exerted by the frugal and archaic elements in Jeffersonian Republicanism and its "Country" antecedents, this rhetoric became increasingly hollow and forced after 1815.[8]

While Europe was in the full tide of post-Revolutionary, post-Napoleonic reaction, the United States was entering a period of political democracy based on white manhood suffrage. How much, or even whether, economic equality was increased is the subject of debate,[9] but there is no doubt about the dominance of egalitarian ideology in political rhetoric. Perhaps more important, egalitarian manners pervaded the culture, offending British visitors and American believers in the lost cause of traditional deference. European models for education and literary culture were placed on the defensive. In America even the top class came quickly to realize, however reluctantly, that it had to live with democracy. This created a sharp contrast with Europe, where some partisans of the old order believed for a long time that they could reverse all that had happened since 1789.

To summarize, in early nineteenth-century America no doctrine or institution could survive that was not compatible with popular Protestantism, expanding capitalism, and political democracy. Contradictions between members of this trinity may bother those who like their intellectual history to be logical. Logical or not—and the combination may really make more sense than it seems to—most Americans believed at once in original sin, political and social equality, and economic expansion.

Under these conditions, what vestiges of the Enlightenment were best able to survive into nineteenth-century America? It is necessary here to disagree with several important historians who believe that America is the place where the program of the philosophes was put into practice.[10] It is hard to imagine Voltaire, Diderot, or Hume—or for that matter Jefferson or Adams—finding much to approve of in Jacksonian America. Yet there were two major survivals from the nation's Enlightened beginnings. One was the system of government, much altered but still based on major Enlightenment doctrines. The other was the belief in the progress of science as a source of future happiness. Republican government and democratic society, early nineteenth-century Americans believed, was certain to produce unprecedented progress in science and all the arts. Until mid-century, most Americans believed that the findings of science would increasingly confirm the truths of revealed religion.[11]

In discussing survivals from the eighteenth century a little further, I hope that the categories I have suggested in my *Enlightenment in America* may be of some use. The earliest form of Enlightenment, the largely British Moderate Enlightenment, the tradition of balance and order that had claimed the devotion of many of the Founding Fathers, declined rapidly despite its enshrinement in the Constitution. So did the closely related tradition of civic humanism so persuasively described by John Pocock and others. However much this tradition may or may not have dominated eighteenth-century America, neither Aristotle, Polybius, Machiavelli nor the later pillars of civic humanism seemed to have much relevance to the ideological needs of an expansive, mostly agrarian, and Protestant society.[12] Some of the followers of Andrew

Jackson, Ward tells us, specifically attacked John Quincy Adams for reading Grotius, Pufendorf, and Vattel.[13]

The Skeptical Enlightenment, never strong in America, was driven underground by religious revival. A few Americans relished Voltaire and Volney in private, and the latent power of these skeptical authors was suggested by endless sermons against their teachings. The Revolutionary Enlightenment presents a more complex case. By the late 1790s fewer and fewer Americans believed in the secular millennium on the Paris model or placed their hopes in its spread through Europe behind French bayonets. Yet many Americans believed in the worldwide revolutionary power of their own version of the democratic millennium. From the most radical Jacksonians on, one after another New Left was to rediscover the power of Rousseau and especially of Paine.

Finally, the Didactic Enlightenment, a defensive adaptation of some of the ideas of the Scottish Common-Sense philosophers, pervaded American higher education and literary culture. In its textbook version, the Scottish Enlightenment was used to fight skepticism and dangerous subjectivism, to support the canons of traditional morality and literary taste, to inculcate the axioms of laissez-faire economics. In the long run, however this bland version of Englightenment was to prove unstable. Its foundations lay in the moral sense, supported by the intuition of mankind. The intuition of mankind is far too dangerous and unreliable a force to serve the purposes of cultural defense.

Bearing in mind American conditions and American survivals, we can begin to see why some European paths out of the Enlightenment were blocked to Americans, others not quite blocked but full of thorns and obstructions. In France, after the years of Revolutionary chaos, Napoleon, in his code of laws and his centralized organization of science and culture, produced something like a new Imperial Enlightenment, purged of subversive elements, controlled and regulated for the national glory. Nothing remotely like this was possible in America, where even Jefferson's mild and inoffensive proposals for government support of science or for a national university were rejected as anti-popular, and the President's own interests in anthropology and geology became favorite subjects for Federalist ridicule.

In France it was possible to transmute much of the heritage of the Skeptical Enlightenment into positivism and various movements of anti-religious social thought, left and right. This process was nearly impossible in ardently Protestant America. In England, much the same heritage emerged in the form of utilitarianism. Though American poets and European critics constantly complained about the crassness and materialism of American society, overtly utilitarian ethics were constantly denounced by the American pulpit and press. American followers of Bentham were very few, and no American was able, in the early nineteenth century, to attract a wide following for secular liberalism on the pattern of Mill.

In both England and France some partisans of the Revolutionary Enlightenment pursued their revolutionary path until Enlightened revolution turned into Romantic revolution. This path led from Rousseau to Godwin to Shelley. Precedents and institutions were the enemies of Enlightenment and Revolution. One must discard all these, and build anew on the only possible remaining foundation: natural goodness. In America a general satisfaction with existing governments and churches, together with surviving Calvinist doubts about human nature, made this path difficult until a special American variant was worked out by Emerson and his friends.

Far more difficult still—indeed almost impossible for

Americans to enter—was the opposite European path, that of Romantic conservatism, love of all that is old and "natural" and organic, suspicion of everything newly and deliberately fashioned. This was the path of Burke in England, and later, in France, of Maistre and Bonald. Only a few eccentric Americans were ever to venture far in this direction.

Somewhat related, the European Romanticism of folk tradition, of ancient lore and song, seemed difficult to adapt to the New World. Irving's experiments with the folklore of Dutch New York wore thin rapidly, and the New England Puritan tradition, until Hawthorne's day, was too close for comfort. Yet Scott, the most respectable of Romantics, proved acceptable even in households where novels were normally prohibited. He opened the way, and by the 1820s Cooper was following it with great success.

The path of Romantic decadence, of reversed morality, at once frightened and attracted Protestant and progressive America. Byron especially was America's favorite shocker. Lyman Beecher, perhaps the most powerful shaper of early nineteenth-century American Protestantism, tearfully lamented in 1824 that the wonderfully gifted poet had died without performing any great work for Christ.[14] Poe, who dared only a little later to experiment with the perverse, notoriously had to find his greatest admirers in Europe.

The least alarming to Americans of major Romantic poets was probably Wordsworth, impeccably pure, at least quasi-religious, and, in his maturity, an enemy of Jacobin revolution. Yet even he and, still more, his friend Coleridge were excluded for some time by the dominant American critics belonging to the Common-Sense school, who had set up a formidable barricade against whatever was incomprehensible, undisciplined, and therefore potentially dangerous.

Finally, it is time to ask what paths were not blocked, and in what forms American Romanticism overcame its many obstacles. One must use a loose definition here, one that covers all kinds of preference for instinct, intuition, or feeling to rational analysis and classical restraint. One must avoid the impossible and not very interesting problem of chickens and eggs, taking account of many subtly related movements that overlapped both in time and content.

For students of this vast cultural earthquake some of the most interesting suggestions have arisen from a newly developed and extraordinarily vital field of history. Let me call this new field the History of the Feelings.[15] This intersects in important ways with the thriving history of women. It is also importantly related to the history of the family, of sexual relations, of attitudes toward death. It clearly has a lot to do with popular religion, popular politics, and popular literature. It has important but less obvious relations with some more traditional kinds of history, including both intellectual and religious history. In America as in Europe, the recognized patron of the new cult of feeling was Rousseau. Much of Rousseau's influence was felt at second hand through new educational theory and, even more powerfully, through the sentimental literature that flourished in the late eighteenth century both in Europe and America. And in America the importance of raised affections had been stated by Jonathan Edwards and vulgarized by many later revivalists.

In the nineteenth century the principal realm for the legitimate expression of feeling was the family. One British historian has said that to hear Victorians talk about the family, one might suppose that it had been invented in the 1830s.[16] In Europe and America, as the classical tradition of civic virtue and public responsibility waned and capitalist competition became more frantic, men

sought refuge in the inviolable private haven of chaste
and permissible emotion.

In this all-important realm women reigned. Women
remained, in the early nineteenth century, officially inferior to men in law, property holding, and politics. The
radical feminism of Mary Wollstonecraft and her followers had been crushed along with the rest of the Revolutionary Enlightenment. Women, on the other hand,
were increasingly conceded superiority in morality and
especially in the newly important qualities of purity,
tenderness, and affection. Small children were handed
over to them to raise, and for many men, religion
gradually tended to become almost a special female
preserve.[17]

This important set of changes, barely sketched here,
may be the central element in the whole cultural change
this article is about. The rise of feeling, of the family,
of expressed emotion is plausibly related by some historians to guilt arising from increased capitalist aggression, barely sanctioned by Enlightened and classical
norms.[18] Others relate it, even more convincingly, to the
dangerous and sometimes uncontrollable emotions
aroused by new kinds of religion.

Shortly before the end of the eighteenth century a
series of religious revivals broke out, mainly at first in
the Eastern states. At first these revivals were under the
control of college-based clergy, mostly moderate Calvinists, followers and modifiers of the theology of the great
Edwards. Soon, however, it became obvious that efforts
to control this burgeoning popular movement were fail-
ing. The center of revivalism shifted from New England
to Tennessee and Kentucky, and from there new kinds
of revival spread all over the country. The important
share of religious exercises assigned by Edwards to the
emotions was expanded beyond all control. Attacks mul-

tiplied against the cold religion of the head, against discouraging and elitist Calvinist theologies, against the very idea of a learned clergy.

This outburst of heart religion constituted the single most powerful attack on the principles and still more on the mental habits associated with the Enlightenment in America.[19] A free, spontaneous, unpracticed style of preaching became the goal of evangelists, and some of them wielded a racy, colloquial, highly personal style with stinging satirical effect. Running sometimes to extremes, religious revival could give rise to wild and uncontrollable emotions, to antinomian heresies and millennial fantasies. Naturally the emotional excesses of revivalist religion frightened many. Popular American religion became the most important source both of American wildness and American repression.

On the middle-class level where popular revivalism was perceived as indecorous, religion was softened and sentimentalized. Doctrines of predestination and reprobation were diluted and explained away.[20] Increasingly, middle-class preachers proclaimed that women were specially formed for religion because of their qualities of heart. Only occasionally preachers, women became increasingly active in church-related organizations, beginning with maternal societies and going on to moral reform groups.[21]

Only among New England intellectuals did the Enlightened compromises with rationalism survive on any important scale. And even in New England Unitarianism, the surviving fortress of the Moderate and Didactic forms of Enlightenment, a place was found for feeling and poetry: for Wordsworth if not for Byron and Goethe.[22]

From this point on, successful American political and social movements became much more like religious revivals than like the Constitutional Convention. Democracy, instead of one of the three classically warranted forms of government, with its strengths and weaknesses like the other two, became the sacred destiny of world history, with America its chosen people. The spread of American democracy became a divinely ordained and therefore inevitable process. Andrew Jackson, as Ward showed us so well, became an inspired, untutored prophet of democracy, to be followed without much regard for his particular policies. Among radicals, movements for social change increasingly moved from the programmatic to the millennial mode.

By this time perhaps we can understand better why New England intellectuals, from about the mid 1830s, were preaching the same basic romantic doctrines as Jacksonian politicians. We have often been told the story of the American discovery of Germany. Brought up on the Scottish Common-Sense thinkers, New England thinkers tended increasingly to discard them. From Schelling and his prophet Coleridge they learned to distinguish between the earthbound Understanding and what Coleridge called Reason, a divinely implanted faculty that enabled the thinker to speak with the voice of Nature and therefore of God. But as Emerson understood particularly well, New England Transcendentalism was not entirely exotic. In large part it welled up from American popular religion and egalitarian culture. The Germans provided a special language for universal truth. Their teachings had to be adapted, and with some difficulty *were* adapted, to conform to essential Protestantism, essential democracy, and the individualistic energies of early capitalism.

Because of the complexities of this adaptation, American Transcendentalism developed fully only a generation after the Revolution. But when it came it amounted to far more than a set of intellectual arguments. Its essential teaching, that the instincts of everyman spoke for God and Nature, was to be rediscovered by American movements both of the right and left in all subsequent periods. And its God, immanent in nature and humanity, took over from the Calvinist deity in the major organizations of American Protestantism.

Romantic philosophy demanded to be expressed in art, and it began to affect American painting remarkably early. Washington Allston was a major prophet, even if a minor (though competent and versatile) painter. Allston was a contemporary of the first generation of Romantic or pre-Romantic painters, of Blake, Turner, and Delacroix. A Bostonian of South Carolinian origin, able to afford long residence in Europe, he became a close friend of Samuel Taylor Coleridge, who considered him a "high and rare genius." Allston was a poet and theorist of Romanticism as well as a painter. Following his teacher Benjamin West, he usually painted in the grand theatrical style. His works included melancholy Swiss or Italian landscapes, often moonlit, and huge Biblical scenes. Allston's work culminated in a gigantic "Belshazzar's Feast" which he was never able to finish. This gave rise, at the time and later, to the familiar picture of an artist frustrated by the sordid and unfeeling American public. Actually Allston was rather more overrated than the reverse, supported by subscriptions and admired by many of the New England intellectuals (though Emerson had some doubts).[23]

In its period of fuller development American Romantic painting did not follow the directions pointed out to it in precept and example by Allston. The most successful work of Romantic painters from the 1830s on, from the Hudson River School through George Inness to Albert Bierstadt usually dealt with American landscape, carefully depicted and heightened or idealized to one degree or another. Perhaps there is some analogy between the "Romantic realism" of these painters and others and Emerson's call, in "The American Scholar," for knowing the "highest spiritual cause lurking, as it always does lurk" in "the meal in the firkin; the milk in the pan; the ballad in the street; the news of the boat; the glance of the eye; the form and gait of the body...."

Finally and most completely, Romantic insight and theory found its way to imaginative literature, usually the dominant and characteristic form of American expression. The full development of American Romantic literature was delayed by the defensive strictures of the Common-Sense critics, who clung to the doctrines of the Didactic Enlightenment, expressing deep and genuine fears of whatever was extreme or irrational. We have recently learned of the existence of a rich subliterature that cheerfully ignored these strictures.[24] In much of the popular press, in penny pamphlets and forgotten popular novels, ignored by critics at the time and forgotten by literary historians, extremes of emotion, all sorts of violence, sado-masochism, and thinly disguised pornography were everyday staples.

For writers who wanted to be taken seriously by critics and intellectuals, for those who longed to contribute to a permanent national literature, boundaries remained strict. Work that clearly transgressed the teachings of Protestant morality, political democracy, and capitalism was beyond the borders. This was true even for those who longed to follow the examples of the new English poets. One should remember that the most widely admired American Romantic poetry was the nostalgic and moralistic work of Longfellow. Even Emerson, who dared to ask his followers to cast aside all conformity and become newborn bards of the Holy Ghost, never quite allowed his muse to lead him clear outside the moral and social boundaries set by his society.

To dare to ask the most dangerous questions is part of what makes great literature. By the middle of the century a few bold and greatly gifted Romantic writers dared this. First Poe, then in quite separate and distinct ways Whitman, Hawthorne, and Dickinson raised questions that took their readers far beyond the boundaries of religious and moral convention. The paradoxes of democracy and capitalism as well as religion and morality were looked at without protective lenses by these writers and most boldly of all by Herman Melville. From this point on the dominant conflict in American literary culture was not between Romanticism and the Enlightenment, but between safe Romanticism and wild Romanticism.

Ralph Waldo Emerson, looking back at New England in the days before the sudden outbreak of Transcendentalist ideas and pronouncements, found it completely dead—without a book or a thought. Harriet Beecher Stowe, in this more imaginative than the Sage of Concord, said it was a time when

> our own hard, rocky, sterile New England was a sort of half Hebrew theocracy, half ultra-democratic republic of little villages, separated by a pathless ocean from all the civilization and refinement of the Old World, forgotten and unnoticed, and yet burning like live coals under this obscurity with all the fervid activity of an intense, newly kindled, peculiar, and individual life.[25]

Between 1830 and 1860 whatever coals had been glowing, in New England and in America, burst into flame. Because Romanticism pervaded every aspect of American culture, from low to high, from politics and religion to literature, it achieved a dominance that the Enlightenment, for all its great figures and lofty doctrines, had never attained. Romanticism dominated America more completely than it did any European country except perhaps Germany. This fact gave American culture much of its great energy. There were also heavy costs to pay. In America all causes tend to become crusades. Around the corner of the sublime lurks the crazy: as Poe and Hawthorne and Melville knew, there is no poetry without danger, no prophecy without potential violence. It is fortunate that America's constitutional system, our main surviving inheritance from the Enlightenment, has so far, often precariously, held its own.

Notes

Introduction: Faith in History

1. I have profited greatly from many discussions of the subject of this introduction with my friends David Hollinger and Fred H. Matthews. Neither is responsible for my opinions or, I suspect, likely to agree with them. I have made minor changes in some of these essays in the interest of increased clarity.

2. I have discussed the origins of this habit of thought in my autobiography, *Coming to Terms* (Berkeley and Los Angeles, 1987), esp. pp. 308 ff.

3. I have found the following especially interesting: Peter Novick, *That Noble Dream: The Objectivity Question and the American Historical Profession* (Cambridge, 1988). David Harlan *et al.*, American Historical Review Forum, "Intellectual History and the Return of Literature," *American Historical Review*, 94 (1988–89): 581–698; David Megill, *Prophets of Extremity* (Berkeley and Los Angeles, 1985). I was also compelled to think about these matters for my reply to criticisms of my *End of American Innocence* in a retrospective session on that book at the 1989 meeting of the Organization of American Historians. The present introduction draws heavily on the remarks I prepared for that occasion.

4. The rather dramatic way I happened to make this discovery is described in *Coming to Terms*, pp. 63–78, and referred to briefly in the note introducing my introduction to Harriet Beecher Stowe's *Oldtown Folks*, below.

5. The effect of Niebuhr on my religious views is discussed in *Coming to Terms*, his effect on my view of history in "Religion

and American Intellectual History," below, his effect on my political thinking and that of my contemporaries in my review of Richard Fox's biography, below.

6. See "The Rough Road to *Virgin Land*," below.

1. Religion and American Intellectual History 1945–1985

1. Ahlstrom, "Theology and the Present-day Religious Revival," *Annals of the American Academy of Political and Social Science*, CCCXXXII (November 1960): 27.

2. This essay is reprinted in my *Ideas, Faiths and Feelings* (New York, 1983), 65–86.

3. Bellah, *Beyond Belief* (New York, 1970), xvii-xviii.

4. Higham, "Beyond Consensus: The Historian as Moral Critic," speech at American Historical Association, 1960, reprinted in *The American Historical Review* in April 1962 and in *Writing American History* (Bloomington, Ind., 1970); quotation, p. 146.

5. Many of the papers given at this conference are reprinted in *New Directions in American Intellectual History*, ed. John Higham and Paul K. Conkin (Baltimore, 1979).

6. Howard R. Bowen and Jack H. Schuster, *American Professors: A Resource Imperiled* (New York, 1986), cited by Andrew Hacker, "The Decline of Higher Learning," *New York Review of Books*, February 13, 1986, p. 38.

7. *New York Review of Books*, February 7, 1986, p. 7.

4. Harriet Beecher Stowe's Oldtown Folks

1. H.B.S. to Fields, 1865. Stowe letters, Huntington Library. The letters in this collection are ordinarily dated only very roughly if at all, except when they are written by Mrs. Stowe's secretary. All letters referred to below and not otherwise identified are in this collection. Quotations are by permission of the Huntington Library.

2. H.B.S. to Fields, 1868.

3. H.B.S. to Fields, "per sect.," February 18, 1869.

4. *Nation,* June 3, 1869, pp. 437–38.

5. *The Overland Monthly,* 3 (1869): 3.

6. The *Nation* review (and the editor's subsequent apology) and also the Natick celebration are discussed in Mrs. Stowe's letter to Annie Fields of May 9, 1869. *Sam Lawson's Oldtime Fireside Stories* was published in 1872.

7. Rourke, *Trumpets of Jubilee* (New York, 1927).

8. Wilson, *Patriotic Gore* (New York, 1963). Midway between these two rediscoveries of Mrs. Stowe, Ruth Suckow, herself a regional novelist and the daughter of a Congregational minister, argued for the importance of the book as a religious novel from a somewhat less anti-Puritan point of view. Suckow, "An Almost Lost American Classic," *College English,* 14 (1952–53): 315–25.

9. Jonathan Edwards, *Images or Shadows of Divine Things,* ed. Perry Miller, (New Haven, 1948), 44.

10. Charles H. Foster, *The Rungless Ladder* (Durham, N.C., 1954), 202.

11. Lowell to H.B.S. February 4, 1859, quoted in Charles Edward Stowe, *The Life of Harriet Beecher Stowe* (Boston, 1889).

12. This daring insight is repeated in Perry Miller's essay, "From Edwards to Emerson," reprinted in his *Errand into the Wilderness* (Cambridge, Mass., 1956), 184–203. It is tempting to speculate whether the first suggestion of it may have come from Miller's highly sympathetic reading of Mrs. Stowe.

13. C. W. Stowe, "Sketches and Recollections of Dr. Lyman Beecher," *Congregational Quarterly,* 23 (1864): 226–29. Mrs. Stowe echoes, in *Oldtown Folks,* her husband's complaint that New England neglects Biblical study for exegesis of Edwards.

14. Quoted in Frank Hugh Foster, *A Genetic History of New England Theology* (Chicago, 1907), 117.

15. Mrs. Stowe's novel makes it clear that this austere notion of virtue was far from a deterrent to action for the improvement of this world. Oliver Wendell Elsbree has pointed out that the Hopkinsian school, acting under this direct injunction to strive after disinterested benevolence, made a distinctive and disproportionately large contribution to several

kinds of New England reform, including antislavery. Elsbree, "Samuel Hopkins and His Doctrine of Benevolence," *New England Quarterly,* 8 (1935): 534–50.

16. There are two editions of Emmons' works. The first, edited by his son-in-law Jacob Ide (6 vols., Boston, 1842), contains in volume 1 Emmons' autobiography. The second, expanded edition (5 vols., Boston, 1863) was re-edited by Edwards Amasa Park, a Calvinist theologian, Andover professor, and friend of Mrs. Stowe. The entire first volume of this edition is a biography of Emmons by Park. This biography, which had been published separately in 1861, is an excellent account of Emmons' life, personality, and doctrine and a neglected source for New England social and religious history.

17. Emmons, *Works* (1842 ed.), VI, 177–89.

18. *Ibid.,* 183.

19. "A celebrated European physician," he said, had calculated that more than half those born in the world die before the age of 8, and even in New England the majority die before reaching 20. Occasionally a whole family survives; as often a whole family is cut down. *Works* (1863 ed.), V, 777–92.

20. *Works* (1842 ed.), I, xxxi-xxxii.

21. *Ibid.,* I, xxxii.

22. The best source for Beecher, and for his children's upbringing, is his *Autobiography,* which is actually a composite work by several of his children, including Harriet, incorporating their father's oral reminiscences recorded by them. The John Harvard Library edition is edited by Barbara Cross (2 vols., Cambridge, Mass., 1961). This can be supplemented by various recollections by contemporaries. For Beecher's theology and that of his closest friend, see Sidney Earl Mead, *Nathaniel William Taylor, 1786–1858* (Chicago, 1942). Beecher's attitude toward Emmons is set forth in the *Autobiography,* I, 374–75.

23. Lyman Beecher Stowe, *Saints, Sinners and Beechers* (Indianapolis, 1934) is a breezy but sometimes informative family history.

24. Florence Thayer McCray, *The Life-Work of the Author of Uncle Tom's Cabin* (New York, 1889), 27.

25. Quoted in Stowe, *Saints, Sinners and Beechers*, 241.

26. Charles E. and Lyman B. Stowe, *Harriet Beecher Stowe* (Boston, 1911), 49. This judgment repeats an earlier one by Charles Stowe. It should be noted that his estimate of the episode's importance meets only qualified agreement in Charles H. Foster's well-informed article, "The Genesis of Harriet Beecher Stowe's 'The Minister's Wooing,' " *New England Quarterly*, 21 (1948): 493–517. The Fisher episode is discussed in the standard Stowe biographies, Lyman Beecher's *Autobiography*, and also at some length in Stowe, *Saints, Sinners and Beechers* and in Elizabeth Harveson, *Catharine Esther Beecher, Pioneer Educator* (Philadelphia, 1932).

27. Beecher, *Autobiography*, I, 355–84.

28. Emmons, *Works* (1842 ed.), III, 246–59.

29. Stowe, *Saints, Sinners and Beechers*, 97. See also Harveson, *Catharine Esther Beecher*.

30. Catharine to Edward Beecher, 1857, quoted in Harveson, p. 99.

31. C. E. Stowe, *Life*, 34.

32. The narrative from which most later accounts of these two conversions are drawn is *ibid.*, 33–52.

33. H.B.S. to Catharine Stowe, undated, quoted *ibid.*, 322.

34. In this section even more than elsewhere I am influenced by the religious interpretation of Mrs. Stowe's entire literary development in Foster's *Rungless Ladder*. I discuss below only those works which seem to me to be directly relevant to *Oldtown Folks*.

35. *Uncle Tom's Cabin* (Boston, 1852), 23.

36. Fields, *Harriet Beecher Stowe* (London, 1898), 376.

37. Stowe, *Sunny Memories of Foreign Lands* (Boston, 1854), II, 353.

38. *Ibid.*, II, 417.

39. *Ibid.*, II, 329.

40. *Ibid.*, II, 359.

41. *Ibid.*, II, 277. This passage is quoted in part in Foster, *Rungless Ladder*, 68.

42. H.B.S. to Catharine Beecher, no date, quoted in C. E. Stowe, *Life*, 322.

43. *Ibid.* It should be pointed out that she attributes this insight partly to a sermon of her husband's.

44. "The Mourning Veil," *Atlantic Monthly,* 1 (1858): 63–70.

45. *Atlantic Monthly,* 1 (1858): 485–92.

46. As Foster shows, Mrs. Stowe characteristically ascribes to her heroine the entire text of a letter from Roxana to Lyman Beecher. The letter expresses Roxana's simple and confident faith in Christ in response to Beecher's Calvinist inquiries. Foster, *Rungless Ladder,* 114–16.

47. *The Minister's Wooing* (Riverside ed.), 274.

48. Lowell to H.B.S., February 4, 1859, quoted in full in C. E. Stowe, *Life,* 333–36.

49. H.B.S. to Mrs. Fields, undated, apparently 1864.

50. C. E. and L. B. Stowe, *Harriet Beecher Stowe,* 278.

51. In her last New England novel, *Poganuc People,* she was to treat Anglicanism more gently and more at length. Here the scene is Litchfield, and the main character a much idealized version of her father, whose battle with the Episcopalians is softened almost beyond recognition. In a fairly acute passage about the various reasons people joined the Episcopal Church, she suggests her own increasingly sentimental attitude toward it: "Then, too, there came to them gentle spirits, cut and bleeding by the sharp crystals of doctrinal statement, and courting the balm of devotional liturgy and the cool shadowy indefiniteness of more aesthetic forms of worship." *Poganuc People* (Boston, 1878), 27.

52. Eleanor M. Tilton, *Amiable Autocrat: A Biography of Dr. Oliver Wendell Holmes* (New York, 1947), 250f.

53. The essay on Edwards can be found in Holmes's *Pages from an Old Volume of Life* (Boston, 1892), 361–401. The best single statement of his religious-philosophical position is probably "Mechanism in Thought and Morals," his Harvard Phi Beta Kappa address of 1870, to be found in the same volume, pp. 260–314. Though not yet delivered when *Oldtown Folks* was being written, this address summarizes long-held views. His biographer believes that a reference in *The Professor at the Breakfast Table* to a "beautiful and affecting letter" from one

whose name "is known to all, in some of its representations" refers to Mrs. Stowe. The letter apparently protests unduly harsh treatment of ministers. Holmes gently stated his respect for the cloth, and then went on to the usual effective attack. Tilton, *Amiable Autocrat*, 250. The number of the *Professor* referred to was originally published in the *Atlantic Monthly*, 3 (1859): 609–20, immediately before a chapter of *The Minister's Wooing*.

54. Foster, *Rungless Ladder*, 131–32.

55. Holmes to H.B.S., May 29, 1867, quoted in John T. Morse, Jr., *Life and Letters of Oliver Wendell Holmes* (2 vols., Boston, 1896), 226.

56. Holmes to H.B.S., no date, *ibid.*, 246.

57. H.B.S. to James B. Fields, August 16, 1868, Stowe papers. Quoted in full with minor inaccuracies by Forrest Wilson, *Crusader in Crinoline* (New York, 1941), 530–31.

58. See Edmund Wilson's essay on Calvin Stowe in *Patriotic Gore*, 59–70.

59. McCray, *Life-Work*, 379.

60. For this purpose the most useful of the biographies is C. E. and L. B. Stowe, *Harriet Beecher Stowe*, esp. pp. 258–60. Local tradition and two early town histories are drawn upon to identify *Oldtown* characters in "The Story of Natick," a pamphlet published by the Natick Federal Savings and Loan Association (Natick, 1948). One of the early histories, Oliver N. Bacon, *A History of Natick* (Boston, 1856), contains "A Brief Account of the Customs and Manners of Living in the Days of Our Forefathers" which, with other material in this book, may have been used by Mrs. Stowe to supplement her husband's reminiscences.

61. Bacon, *Natick*, 66. An earlier history makes him both an Arminian and a Unitarian, adding that he thought it politic to conceal the latter belief. William Biglow, *History of the Town of Natick* (Boston, 1830), 61.

62. Elias Nason, *Sir Charles Frankland, Baronet, or Boston in the Colonial Times* (Albany, 1865).

63. For instance the preparation of pies for Thanksgiving, and freezing them for use all winter. *Autobiography*, I, 15.

64. Mrs. Stowe's reminiscences of "Nutplains" are in Lyman Beecher's *Autobiography,* I, 228–34.

65. The best sources on Litchfield Female Academy, in addition to the standard Stowe material, are Alain C. White, *The History of the Town of Litchfield, Connecticut, 1720–1920* (Litchfield, 1920), and Elizabeth C. Barney Buel, ed., *The Chronicles of a Pioneer School* (Cambridge, Mass., 1903), which puts together a mass of primary material. Both are supplemented by Harveson, *Catharine Esther Beecher,* and by descriptions of the school by both Catharine and Harriet Beecher in their father's *Autobiography,* I, 164–66, 397–99.

66. The essay is printed in full in C. E. Stowe, *Life,* 15–21.

67. *Autobiography,* I, 179, 238–39.

68. H.B.S. to Fields, March 2, 1869. Stowe papers. Her injunction was followed in her next book, *Sam Lawson's Oldtown Fireside Stories.*

69. For estimates of Mrs. Stowe's position in the local color movement, see Walter Blair, *Native American Humor* (New York, 1937); Perry D. Westbrook, *Acres of Flint* (Washington, 1961); and Richard M. Dorson, *Jonathan Draws the Long Bow* (Cambridge, Mass., 1946).

70. Lydia H. Sigourney, *Sketch of Connecticut Forty Years Since* (Hartford, 1824), 116. Mrs. Sigourney was a Hartford author, and probably known personally by Harriet Beecher during her first Hartford stay. Catharine Beecher wrote her asking help in promoting her treatise on Domestic Economy: see Harveson, *Catharine Esther Beecher,* 77. Mrs. Stowe certainly read Mrs. Sigourney, and borrowed as was her custom. A pair of twins in the *Sketch* are called Roxy and Ruey, the names used for the two old maids in *The Pearl of Orr's Island.*

71. Foster considers this book her most artistic performance, *Rungless Ladder,* 218.

72. For a highly interesting discussion of this phase of Mrs. Stowe's career, in which the relation between her work and Mark Twain's is discussed at length, see Kenneth R. Andrews, *Nook Farm, Mark Twain's Hartford Circle* (Cambridge, Mass., 1950).

73. For an authoritative discussion of Mark Twain's formal

and colloquial styles and their significance, see Henry Nash Smith, *Mark Twain, the Development of a Writer* (Cambridge, Mass., 1962).

5. Jonathan Edwards and America

1. M. X. Lesser, *Jonathan Edwards: A Reference Guide* (Boston, 1981), xli. This volume has assisted me greatly in preparing this keynote.

2. Samuel Hopkins, *The Life and Character of the Late Reverend Mr. Jonathan Edwards* (1765), in David Levin, ed., *Jonathan Edwards, A Profile* (New York, 1969), 1–2.

3. The latest, and one of the best, contributions to this long debate is Joseph Conforti, *Samuel Hopkins and the New Divinity* (Grand Rapids, 1981). See especially pp. 175–90.

4. Timothy Dwight, *The Triumph of Infidelity*, quoted by Lesser, *Jonathan Edwards*, 46.

5. *The Autobiography of Lyman Beecher*, ed. Barbara M. Cross (2 vols., Cambridge, Mass., 1961), I, 46.

6. E. A. Park, "The Duties of a Theologian," *American Biblical Repository*, Second Series (1840), 374.

7. John Adams to John Taylor, 1814, reprinted in Adrienne Koch, ed., *The American Enlightenment* (New York, 1965), 222.

8. Oliver Wendell Holmes, "Jonathan Edwards," in *Pages from an Old Volume of Life* (Boston, 1892), 392–402.

9. Harriet Beecher Stowe, *Oldtown Folks*, ed., Henry F. May (Cambridge, Mass., 1966), 401.

10. Clemens to the Reverend J.H. Twichell, February 1902, in A. B. Paine, *Mark Twain's Letters* (2 vols., New York, 1917), II, 719–20.

11. See Norman Fiering, *Jonathan Edwards' Moral Thought and Its British Context* (Chapel Hill, 1981), 200–260.

12. Holmes to Stowe, May 29, 1867, quoted in H. May, Introduction to *Oldtown Folks*, above, 107.

13. V. L. Parrington, *Main Currents of American Thought* (3 vols., New York, 1927, 1930), I, 162–63.

14. Henry Bamford Parkes, *Jonathan Edwards. The Fiery Puritan* (New York, 1930), 254.

15. Jonathan Edwards, "Freedom of the Will," ed. Paul Ramsey (New Haven, 1957), 437.

16. Fiering, *Edwards' Moral Thought*, 148.

17. Perry Miller, *Jonathan Edwards* (New York), 176.

18. Cambridge, Mass., 1966.

19. Reinhold Niebuhr, *Moral Man and Immoral Society* (New York, 1960; first ed., 1932), 67.

20. H.R. Niebuhr, "Ex Libris," *The Christian Century*, June 13, 1962, p. 754.

21. Joseph Haroutunian, *Piety versus Moralism* (New York, 1932; paperback ed., 1970), xxxii-xxxiii.

22. Conrad Cherry, *The Theology of Jonathan Edwards* (New York, 1966), 6.

23. John E. Smith, introduction to Edwards, *Religious Affections*, reprinted in Levin, ed., *Jonathan Edwards*, 211, 217.

24. C.C. Goen, "Jonathan Edwards: A New Departure in Eschatology," *Church History*, XXXVIII (1959): 25–40; Stephen J. Stein, introduction to Jonathan Edwards, *Apocalyptic Writings* (New Haven, 1977).

25. Fiering, *Edwards' Moral Thought*, 97.

26. Parrington, *Main Currents*, I, 152.

27. Edwards, "The Excellency of Christ," in C.H. Faust and Thomas H. Johnson, *Jonathan Edwards, Representative Selections* (New York, 1925; paperback ed., 1962), 125.

28. Fiering, *Edward's Moral Thought*, 361, 292.

29. James Hoopes, "Jonathan Edwards' Religious Psychology," *The Journal of American History*, LXIX (1982–83): 861.

30. Edwards, "A Divine and Supernatural Light," in Faust and Johnson, eds., *Jonathan Edwards*, 102.

6. The Constitution and the Enlightened Consensus

1. Robert Wiebe, however, finds "no basic ideological conflict" among the "gentry" who governed early America. *The Opening of American Society* (New York, 1984), xiii.

2. J. G. A. Pocock, "Virtue and Commerce in the Eighteenth Century," *Journal of Interdisciplinary History*, III (1972): 119–34.

3. See W. W. Sweet, *Religion in the Development of American Culture* (New York, 1942), 85. Sweet finds only one deist, but I think this underestimates the number who held essentially deist convictions.

4. Morton G. White, a thoroughly secular-minded writer, says, "I do not think that the authors [of *The Federalist*] could have defended their version of natural rights without some appeal to a Creator of man's essence even though the references to God in *The Federalist* are quite exiguous and perfunctory." *Philosophy, The Federalist, and the Constitution* (New York, 1987), 206. I agree with Patricia Bonomi's comment on historical conventions when she says that "an eighteenth century of 'Enlightenment' skepticism coming between a 'Puritan' seventeenth century and an 'evangelical' nineteenth century simply does not add up." *Under the Cope of Heaven* (New York, 1986), 220. Historians who have subscribed to this periodization have usually been discussing quite different groups of people. Another excellent recent book warns against "the tendency to prematurely secularize the thought of allegedly 'modern' thinkers." Duncan Forbes, *Hume's Philosophical Politics* (Cambridge, 1975; paperback ed., 1985), fn. 1, p. 61.

5. In Max Farrand, ed., *The Records of the Federal Convention* (New Haven, 1937; paperback ed., 4 vols., 1966), I, 512–13. It should probably be pointed out that Morris was more skeptical than most of the delegates, but in this statement I think he is representative.

6. See White, *Philosophy*, 193–207.

7. *The Federalist* (ed. Jacob E. Cooke), 238, quoted by White, *Philosophy*, 206.

8. This point is brilliantly made by Daniel W. Howe, "The Political Psychology of *The Federalist*," *William and Mary Quarterly*, 3rd series, XLIV (1987): 485–509.

9. See White, *Philosophy*, for instance, p. 38.

10. Despite the admiration of some delegates for Hume, like many Americans they accepted his political essays more

readily than his epistemology. Few if any followed him in thinking the passions a better guide than reason.

11. Jefferson to Samuel Kercheval, July 12, 1816, in *Works*, ed. P. L. Ford (New York, 1904–05), XII, 11–12.

12. Tocqueville, *Democracy in America*, ed. Phillips Bradley (2 vols., New York, 1945), I, 58–59.

13. Tocqueville, *Democracy*, II, 352.

7. The Enlightenment and America: The Jeffersonian Moment

1. Peter Gay, chapter on "The Program in Practice," *The Enlightenment: An Interpretation*, II, 555–68. Henry Steele Commager, *The Empire of Reason: How Europe Imagined and America Realized the Enlightenment* (Garden City, N.Y., 1977).

2. I have argued the reality of the Enlightenment at more length in "The Problem of the American Enlightenment," *New Literary History*, I (1970): 201–14, reprinted in my *Ideas, Faiths, and Feelings* (New York, 1983), 111–29.

3. Henry Vyverberg, *Historical Pessimism in the French Enlightenment* (Cambridge, Mass., 1958).

4. René Pomeau, *L'Europe des Lumières* (Paris, 1960), quoted in *Le Monde*, June 15, 1985.

5. Quoted in Gay, *The Enlightenment*, II, 521. On the limits of Enlightenment egalitarianism see Harvey Chisick, *The Limits of Reform in the Enlightenment* (Princeton, 1981).

6. John Adams, *A Defense of the Constitutions of Government of the United States of America*, selections in Adrienne Koch and William Peden, eds., *The Selected Writings of John and John Quincy Adams* (New York, 1946), 83.

7. Thomas Jefferson to John Adams, October 28, 1813, *The Works of Thomas Jefferson*, ed. P. L. Ford (New York, 1904–05), xi, 343–44.

8. Jefferson, "Notes on Virginia," *Works*, IV, 61.

9. Jefferson, draft of "A Bill for the More General Diffusion of Knowledge," Julian P. Boyd, ed., *The Papers of Thomas Jefferson* (22 vols., Princeton, 1950–86), II, 526.

10. "Bill for Diffusion," *Papers*, II, 528.

Notes

11. Henry F. May, *The Enlightenment in America* (New York, 1976), 153–76.

12. Plumb, in *New York Review of Books,* November 10, 1983, p. 26.

13. Among the scholars I refer to here are Ernest Tuveson, Norman Cohn, Nathan Hatch, and James West Davidson. The fullest treatment of millennialism and its political interpretation in early America is Ruth Bloch, *Visionary Republic, Millennial Themes in American Thought: 1756–1800* (Cambridge, Mass., 1985).

14. Anthony Lincoln, *Some Political and Social Ideas of English Dissent, 1763–1800* (Cambridge, Eng., 1938).

15. Sidney Mead, "American Protestantism during the Revolutionary Epoch," in *The Lively Experiment* (1963), 38–54.

16. Jefferson, "Notes on Virginia," *Works,* IV, 78.

17. This can be seen as a victory of the Revolutionary Enlightenment over the earlier Moderate Enlightenment, since many of the Anglican clergy and their supporters belonged to the latter camp.

18. "Notes on Virginia," *Works,* IV, 81–82.

19. Quoted by editor in *Papers,* II, 552.

20. Quoted by editor in *Papers,* II, 546, 649. The case that the Statute as written did not protect freedom of opinion is made by Walter Berns, "Religion and the Founding Principle," in Robert H. Horwitz, ed., *The Moral Foundations of the American Republic* (Charlottesville, 1979), 157–82.

21. Comments by editor in *Papers,* II, 550–51; Dumas Malone, *Jefferson and the Rights of Man* (Boston, 1951), 279.

22. Gordon S. Wood, "The Democratization of Mind in the American Revolution," in Horwitz, ed., *Moral Foundations,* 103.

23. Joyce Appleby, *Capitalism and a New Social Order: The Republican Vision* (New York, 1984).

24. Joseph Ellis, *The Jeffersonian Crisis: Courts and Politics in the Young Republic* (New York, 1971).

25. May, *Enlightenment,* 311–12.

26. Jefferson to Lafayette, February 14, 1815, *Works,* XI, 456.

27. Jefferson to John Taylor, May 28, 1816, *Works*, XI, 532.

8. After the Enlightenment: A Prospectus

1. John William Ward, *Andrew Jackson: Symbol for an Age* (New York, 1953), 50.
2. *Ibid.*, 213.
3. Gordon S. Wood, *The Rising Glory of America* (New York, 1971), 9.
4. Alaisdair MacIntyre, *After Virtue: A Study in Moral Theory* (Notre Dame, 1981) is an excellent summary of this tradition and, with modifications, a powerful statement of it.
5. Peter Gay, *The Enlightenment: An Interpretation*, vol. II, *The Science of Freedom* (New York, 1969), 517–28. See also Harvey Chisick, *The Limits of Reform in the Enlightenment: Attitudes Toward the Education of the Lower Classes in Eighteenth-Century France* (Princeton, 1981).
6. See Carl Becker, "The Dilemma of Diderot," in *Everyman His Own Historian* (New York, 1935), 262–83.
7. E. J. Hobsbawm, *The Age of Revolution, 1789–1848* (New York, 1962), juxtaposes these two events in an interesting manner.
8. Two excellent treatments of socio-economic changes in the post-Revolutionary era are Drew R. McCoy, *The Elusive Republic: Political Economy in Jeffersonian America* (Chapel Hill, 1980) and Steven Watts, *The Republic Reborn: War and the Making of Liberal America, 1790–1820* (Baltimore, 1987). Joyce Appleby, *Capitalism and a New Social Order* (New York, 1984), denies that the Jeffersonian program ever contained any important backward-looking elements.
9. See Edward Pessen, *Riches, Class, and Power Before the Civil War* (Lexington, Mass., 1973).
10. The most unequivocal statement of this belief comes from Henry Steele Commager, who says that in America " . . . the Enlightenment not only survived but triumphed." Commager, *The Empire of Reason: How Europe Imagined and America Realized the Enlightenment* (New York, 1977), xii. Donald H.

Meyer, more circumspectly, finds that the ideals of the Enlightenment were among the ingredients that went into the making of an American faith. Meyer, *The Democratic Enlightenment* (New York, 1976), 213. Peter Gay calls his short chapter on American "The Program [of the philosophes] in Practice." But in this chapter he shows mainly that Enlightened Europeans *believed* that this was the case. Gay, *Science of Reason*, 555–68.

11. See Herbert Hovencamp, *Science and Religion in America 1800–1860* (Philadelphia, 1978).

12. Watts, *Republic Reborn*, convincingly traces the decline of civic republicanism and values associated with this tradition. John P. Diggins questions whether these values were *ever* very important in America. Diggins, *The Lost Soul of American Politics: Virtue, Self-Interest and the Foundations of Liberalism* (New York, 1984). In my opinion the best balanced discussion of this question, and an excellent summary of early American ideology, is James T. Kloppenberg, "The Virtues of Liberalism: Christianity, Republicanism, and Ethics in Early American Political Discourse," *Journal of American History*, 74 (1987–88): 9–33.

13. Ward, *Jackson*, 63, 66.

14. *The Autobiography of Lyman Beecher*, (ed. Barbara M. Cross 2 vols., Cambridge, Mass., 1961), II, 393.

15. Of the books I have read in this field that deal with this period I have learned most from three: Jay Fliegelman, *Prodigals and Pilgrims: The American Revolution Against Patriarchal Authority, 1750–1800* (Cambridge, Eng., 1982); Jan Lewis, *The Pursuit of Happiness: Family and Values in Jefferson's Virginia* (Cambridge, Eng., 1983); and Stephen Watts, *The Republic Reborn* (cited in n. 8 above). Of these, Fliegelman is the most wide-ranging and comes closest to bringing together the whole field and relating it to literary scholarship. The book, however, makes some connections I cannot quite accept. Lewis is the most completely successful of the three authors, and describes affective changes in Virginian planter society in a way that seems to me entirely convincing. Watts argues impressively that the War of 1812 marks a climax in the emotional as well

as in the economic and political history of the Republic, thus giving this war a significance something like that given to major later wars by other historians. Philip Greven, *The Protestant Temperament: Patterns of Child-Rearing, Religious Experience, and the Self in Early America* (New York, 1977), deals creatively with what he sees as enduring types of family patterns rather than with changes over time.

16. William L. Burn, *The Age of Equipoise* (London, 1964), cited in Joseph F. Kett, *Rites of Passage: Adolescence in America, 1790 to the Present* (New York, 1977), 79.

17. For women's gains and losses in this period, see for instance Carl Degler, *At Odds: Women and the Family in America from the Revolution to the Present* (New York, 1980) and Nancy Cott, *The Bonds of Womanhood: 'Woman's Sphere' in New England, 1780–1835* (New Haven, 1977). For the important and surprisingly new doctrine of women's superior sexual purity, see Cott, "Passionlessness: An Interpretation of Victorian Sexual Ideology, 1790–1850," in *Signs,* IV (1978): 219–33, and Ruth Bloch, "The Gendered Meanings of Virtue in Revolutionary America," *Signs,* XIII (1987): 37–58.

18. This point is especially well argued by Watts, *The Republic Reborn.*

19. Of course American religion had already been changed in some of these directions by the Great Awakening of the mid-eighteenth century. Yet in the earlier movement most of the religious energies of revivalism were—however precariously—contained within existing structures and related to an intellectually powerful theology. The great figure of this containment was Jonathan Edwards. No comparable intellectual feat emerged from the Revival of 1800, sometimes called the Second Great Awakening, much of which was specifically and strongly anti-Calvinist as well as anti-intellectual. In a longer development of my present essay I would probably concede that there are, in the American eighteenth century, antecedents for many of the developments I find in the later period, contained by gentry prestige, college-taught rationalism, and Calvinist intellectuality. Thus the changes of the later period, especially in religion but elsewhere as well, can often be seen

as liberations of subdominant tendencies and only partly as brand-new departures. This is how intellectual history ordinarily proceeds.

20. One should not, however, forget the existence of important pockets where Calvinism long survived. In particular, an important group of seminary-based theologians stuck doggedly to intellectually rigorous forms of Calvinist theology. Bruce Kuklick argues that this group exerted a major influence on American thought throughout the nineteenth century. Kuklick, *Churchmen and Philosophers: From Jonathan Edwards to John Dewey* (New Haven, 1985).

21. Cott, *Bonds of Womanhood*, chap. 4, gives an excellent account of women's increasing share in religious activity. Ann Douglas, *The Feminization of American Culture* (New York, 1977) contains a great deal of interesting material on this subject but is impaired by a lack of attention to class levels and denominational boundaries.

22. See Daniel Walker Howe, *The Unitarian Conscience: Harvard Moral Philosophy, 1805–1861* (Cambridge, Mass., 1970), e.g., 200–201.

23. See Edgar P. Richardson, *Washington Allston: A Study of the Romantic Artist in America* (Chicago, 1948). I have found this and Richardson's other writings on American Romantic painting especially helpful, partly because the author makes a serious effort to relate his subject both to European art and to American literature.

24. See David Reynolds, *Beneath the American Renaissance: The Subversive Imagination in the Age of Emerson and Melville* (New York, 1988).

25. Harriet Beecher Stowe, *Oldtown Folks* (Boston, 1869; John Harvard Library Edition, ed. H. F. May, 1966), 49.

Index

Index